CONTENTS

A **Teaching** Profession for the **21st Century**

Volume 1: Report

Introduction

1.1 The independent Committee of Inquiry into Professional Conditions of Service for Teachers was set up on the initiative of Sam Galbraith MSP, the Minister for Children and Education, at the end of September 1999. Its establishment was a response to the breakdown in negotiations on pay and conditions of service between local authority employers and teaching unions in the Scottish Joint Negotiating Committee (SJNC), following the wide-ranging Millennium Review into public education in Scotland which they had jointly carried out in 1997-98. At the same time, Mr Galbraith announced the Executive's intention to remove the statutory backing of the SJNC.

1.2 The Committee's remit was to inquire widely into *"how teachers' pay, promotion structures and conditions of service should be changed in order to ensure a committed, professional and flexible teaching force which will secure high and improving standards of school education for all children in Scotland into the new Millennium; and the future arrangements for determining teachers' pay and conditions in Scotland following the removal of the statutory basis of the Scottish Joint Negotiating Committee proposed by the Scottish Executive."* (The full terms of reference can be found at the end of this report.)

1.3 In the course of its inquiry, the Committee has consulted very widely. Copies of its consultation document were sent to every school, school board and parent teacher organisation in Scotland; to local authority employers and teaching unions; to Members of the Scottish Parliament; and to every organisation with an interest in Scottish education. The document was also produced in Gaelic, and in audio, Braille and large print formats; and it was made freely available via the Internet in English, Gaelic, Urdu, Cantonese, Hindi, Arabic, Punjabi and Bengali. The Committee undertook a programme of fourteen visits to widely differing schools, from Shetland to the Borders, to listen at first hand to the views of teachers, support staff, parents and children; and it took oral evidence from a number of the main organisations involved in Scottish education. (Details can be found at Appendix D of this report.)

1.4 The response to our consultation exercise was impressive. We received nearly 2,600 written submissions, from all parts of Scotland, the great majority of them from individual teachers. (This compares with about 950 submissions to the last such inquiry, carried out in 1986 by Sir Peter Main; or with about 700 submissions to the recent Committee of Inquiry into Student Finance chaired by Andrew Cubie.) The scale of this response is clearly an indication of the depth of feeling about the current situation in Scotland's schools. (The analysis of responses is summarised at Appendix E.)

1.5 Finally, in order to inform its deliberations the Committee commissioned independent and authoritative research into how teachers' pay has fared compared with that for other professions over the past quarter of a century; and, separately, into how teachers' pay currently compares with that for other occupations requiring similar skills and competences, both in the public and the private sectors; and gathered a broad range of statistical information about the Scottish teaching profession. (These projects are described in Appendices A, C and F.)

1.6 The consultation process revealed, as one might expect, a number of differences across

Scotland and across different sectors of the education service, but a greater number of common themes emerged. Teaching is a profession under pressure. Teachers feel that the number and nature of recent policy initiatives by the government – many of them laudable in themselves - have substantially increased the burden upon them. Everywhere the Committee went, the message was the same: that these initiatives were becoming overwhelming. This must be recognised and taken into account. Teachers also feel that the amount of bureaucracy involved in teaching more generally has grown beyond reasonable proportions, and question whether all of it really adds value. They think that the policy of social inclusion has brought with it new demands which exceed the accompanying increase in school resources. And they point to a growing problem of pupil indiscipline in some schools, which is both resource-intensive and stressful.

1.7   More broadly, many in the teaching profession feel misunderstood and under-valued. They think that the public at large does not understand the stresses and strains involved in teaching in an increasingly difficult environment, in which it is felt that parents are more challenging towards teachers than they used to be. In fact, many teachers feel that society as a whole no longer holds teaching in high esteem, and that they are both overworked and underpaid.

1.8   This situation appears to be having a profoundly negative effect on teachers' morale and well-being. Some older teachers say that they would like to leave the profession, but are barred from doing so because of financial constraints on early retirement. Since teaching is, in any case, an ageing profession – over half of Scottish teachers are over 45 years old, and over a quarter are over 50 - this will present a particular challenge to the education service in the years to come. Moreover, there are some worrying signs that the current situation may be having an effect on the number of high-quality graduates entering the profession and remaining there, although the evidence for this is as yet rather unclear. The Committee views these developments with concern.

1.9   On the other hand, the Committee has been impressed throughout its inquiry by the levels of commitment and sheer hard work evident among Scotland's teachers. The great majority of teachers we met were energetic, dedicated professionals performing an excellent job, often in demanding circumstances. We are firmly of the view that most teachers are doing an extremely good job for Scotland's children.

1.10   Against this background of professionalism, the Committee was struck by the extent to which teachers' salaries, allowances, duties, hours of work and other conditions of service were laid down in a very detailed and prescriptive manner in a scheme whose provisions have statutory effect. This level of prescription does not easily lend itself to the flexibility which the education system will need for the future. In our view, the teaching profession of the twenty-first century needs a more flexible, collegial framework if it is to rise to the challenges it faces: but the profession must also be able to count on better support, on the provision of high-quality training and development, and on a career and salary structure which recognises and rewards excellence. These are the key themes we address in this report.

1.11   One specific issue which has been raised a number of times with the Committee is the question of how any changes to pay, promotion structures and conditions of service it may recommend will be financed. The terms of reference drawn up for the Committee by the Scottish Executive asked the Committee, *inter alia*, to *"have regard to public expenditure issues including affordability"*: but the Committee has not been given any clear guidance on what, in practical terms, is to be understood by "affordability".

1.12 The Committee is conscious of the constraints on public expenditure generally and of the arrangements by which public expenditure is allocated to Scotland in particular. The bulk of the funding available to the Executive comes in the form of the Block, which includes expenditure on education. Expenditure per head of population on education in Scotland is at present some 30 per cent above the level in England; Scotland has more teachers per head of population; and the average class size is smaller. This situation is the outcome of past expenditure decisions, and in part this can be explained by the sparsity of population in rural areas. There are qualifications that have to be made to comparisons of this kind, such as the larger number of pupils at private schools in England; and of course there are also significant differences between the English regions. But the essential point is that the 'Barnett Formula', which is now used to allocate changes in public expenditure, simply results in Scotland getting its population share of whatever increases or decreases are made in England. This has two important consequences: first, increased resources are only available to the Scottish Executive if there is increased spending in England; and second, since Scottish spending per head is above the English level now, the application of the formula will gradually bring Scottish expenditure closer to that of England.

1.13 The Scottish Executive is, of course, free to allocate expenditure within the Block as it chooses, but that means that a decision to spend more on education is at the expense of something else; and since education and health are by far the largest components of the Block, the scope for this is limited.

1.14 These matters are, however, for the Executive. The Committee is independent and its task is to put forward recommendations that fulfil the remit given to it by the Minister. We have sought to do this, while retaining a sense of responsibility as regards cost. But our recommendations will require significant additional funds. We consider that inescapable, if we are to put the teaching profession on a sound basis for the new century and improve the quality of school education in Scotland.

Section 2:
Education and the economy

2.1　Scotland's future prosperity depends crucially on the skills of its people – the people educated in Scottish schools. The Scottish economy has changed beyond all recognition in the last few decades; and the nature of the workforce required by the modern Scottish economy, and Scottish society more generally, is very different from that required a generation ago.

2.2　The heavy industries which were the mainstay of our economy until the 1960s, and which remained important until the 1980s – coal, steel, shipbuilding – have contracted dramatically. The heavy engineering and textiles sectors are nowadays employing only a small fraction of their former numbers. Manufacturing now accounts for a much smaller share of the economy. The new industries which have emerged are largely based on finance, other services or the applications of rapidly changing technology - electronics, pharmaceuticals, biotechnology. The modern economy is a high-skill "knowledge economy": there is far less demand for unskilled labour. The increasing globalisation of economic activity has intensified international competition, and reinforced the demand for high-skilled workers.

2.3　Economists agree that in the last few decades the Scottish economy has suffered from serious deficiencies on the supply side. They emphasise the role that skills and knowledge play in determining our competitiveness, and compare our recent record unfavourably with our major international competitors in a number of respects, particularly numeracy and literacy. If these deficiencies were to go uncorrected, they argue, this would tend to drive the Scottish economy towards a low-skill, low-productivity workforce.

2.4　Moreover, the whole nature of work is changing fast. It seems increasingly likely that, instead of pursuing a single career with one organisation for the whole of their working life, more and more people will work for a variety of different employers in the course of their careers, quite possibly in widely differing areas of activity. More people will probably work for themselves, or in less conventional organisational structures than in the past; with the rapid development of information and communication technology, increasing numbers of people may work from home.

2.5　Against this background, the skills with which young people leave Scotland's schools are of critical importance. The successful employee will increasingly be the person who is comfortable with technology; has good communication skills; can adapt quickly; and can work flexibly. Underpinning these competences must be high levels of numeracy and literacy. Delivery of these skills presents a formidable challenge for the Scottish education service.

2.6　Scottish education has a proud tradition, and has many strengths. In particular, it can pride itself on the fact that 48 per cent of Scottish school leavers go on to further or higher education – a significantly better record than the rest of the UK; and that our brightest and best pupils have risen to positions of prominence in industry and government unmatched by the other home nations. However, there are still weaknesses. Too many young people leave school with few or no formal qualifications: 6.6 per cent of school leavers gain no qualifications at all, and a further 14.3 per cent gain only one or two Standard Grades at levels 1 - 3. Levels of attainment in mathematics in Scotland are significantly below the OECD average, and below those of many of our European counterparts. We also lag behind a number of our competitors in literacy skills. Recent reports suggest weaknesses in the area of modern languages – a key requirement if Scotland is to be able to compete within Europe and beyond. And the lack of craft and technician skills has become a weakness which can be seen in labour shortages whenever the Scottish economy is faring particularly well.

2.7 We must remove these weaknesses if Scotland is to be able to compete successfully, and if her economy is to prosper. That means that our objective should be to have an education service second to none. In order to achieve this, we need high-quality, trained, professional, motivated and contented teachers; and we need to restore public esteem for the teaching profession.

Section 3:
Developing and supporting the teaching profession

3.1 Teachers are a valuable resource. Their training represents a major investment not only by themselves as individuals but by the taxpayer. It is therefore important that their skills be developed to enable them to achieve their maximum potential and used to the best advantage in the education of our young people. This means that teachers should primarily be engaged in teaching, the calling for which they have been trained, and in other education-related work in their schools, rather than in a multiplicity of tasks that others could do equally well.

3.2 This section of the report therefore considers the importance of a teacher's initial training and continuing professional development (CPD); it then looks at ways in which the profession should be supported so as to achieve the best use of a teacher's skills. Improving the training and support available to teachers should both improve the quality of teaching and learning and increase the overall cost-effectiveness of our education system.

PROFESSIONAL DEVELOPMENT

Initial training

3.3 To gain a qualification to teach, teachers in Scotland take either a four-year education degree or, for those who already hold a degree in another subject, a one-year course leading to a teaching qualification. In the course of its visits to schools, the Committee had an opportunity to discuss the adequacy of these qualifications as a preparation for teaching with a number of new entrants to the profession. The courses themselves are not strictly within our terms of reference and we therefore did not visit the institutions themselves or attempt a proper appraisal of course content. But initial training closely affects matters that are our concern, and we considered the comments made to be important.

3.4 Some of the teachers to whom we spoke criticised aspects of the initial training they had received. They said that insufficient attention was given to topics such as behaviour management of difficult and aggressive pupils and to the understanding of problems such as attention deficit disorder. It was thought that an insufficient number of the lecturing staff in the teacher education institutions (TEIs) had had recent experience of working in a school, and that they were therefore sometimes out of touch with recent curriculum developments and the problems and requirements of the job as it is now. On the other hand, periods of placement were seen as extremely valuable, especially where these were well organised and where the trainee was given appropriate help and guidance from experienced staff in the schools.

3.5 The talent of young teachers needs to be carefully developed and fostered and they need to be well prepared for the task that lies ahead of them. To find oneself in front of a class for the first time must be a testing experience. The Committee would wish to see teachers starting their careers fully equipped with both the theoretical knowledge of learning and teaching and the skills with which to put this into practice in the classroom.

The Committee is aware that the Scottish Executive, together with other interested parties, has been giving consideration to a number of issues relating to initial training in the light of the Sutherland report on teacher education and training. *In that context, it recommends that the Executive commission a review of the design of initial training courses, and specifically:*

- *that more attention should be given in courses to issues of pupil management, to putting the theories of teaching and learning into practice and to other new needs such as the impact of new technologies and the teaching of modern languages in primary schools;*

- *that TEI staff should be required to update their experience with periodic spells in a school teaching environment as appropriate;*

- *and that schools chosen for teacher placements must have departments where good practice is the norm and where sufficient support and guidance can be given to trainees. The Executive, in conjunction with the other interested parties, should consider drawing up a list of accredited schools and departments for this purpose and allocating them additional funding.*

Probation

3.6   No amount of pre-service training can fully prepare newly qualified entrants for the challenges they will face when they become teachers. The probation period between the time when a teacher gets a provisional registration with the General Teaching Council (GTC) and full GTC registration, which should normally be after satisfactory completion of two years of employment, is therefore of major importance in further developing a teacher's skills. This period should therefore be regarded as an extension of training to enable newly qualified teachers to develop their skill in an appropriate learning environment with the help and guidance of experienced staff.

3.7   The Committee was dismayed to discover that in far too many cases newly qualified teachers received quite inadequate support throughout this period. While some new teachers praised the help they had been given in their probationary period and quickly secured permanent employment, others were given little guidance and could find themselves teaching in a multiplicity of schools on a supply basis. This gave them insufficient opportunity to get to know either the pupils or the staff with whom they were working; they received little in the way of mentoring support or guidance; and it could mean that the probationary period took longer than two years. The Committee views this situation as little short of scandalous. It is no way to treat a new entrant to any profession, let alone one that is as demanding and of such public importance as teaching, where help and wise counsel are essential. It is difficult to think of circumstances more likely to lead to discouragement and to new recruits leaving the profession for other jobs.

3.8   The Committee understands that the Scottish Executive has set a number of measures in train to develop an improved introduction to the profession for newly qualified teachers, including the development of a competence framework for full registration in the context of its approach to CPD (see below). It welcomes this development. *In addition however, it recommends:*

- *that local authority employers should offer probationers at least a full year of stable employment, involving a strictly limited number of placements, rather than using them for intermittent supply;*

- *and that schools should be identified that are able to provide the appropriate support and induction for newly qualified entrants to the profession. Consideration should be given to the idea of designating some schools across the country as "training schools", working in close partnership with TEIs to deliver, on a regional basis, a high-quality and structured introduction to the profession, both during initial training and thereafter. Such an initiative would clearly have resource implications.*

Temporary contracts

3.9   Related to this issue is the problem of temporary contracts. Several teachers told us that, although they had been teaching for a number of years, they had still not been able to get a permanent contract; and some only had temporary employment for that part of the year which excluded school holidays. Invariably this applies to younger teachers: but it may extend for several years beyond probation. While it can be understood that local authorities are up against financial pressure and wish to retain flexibility, this situation is profoundly unsatisfactory and discouraging. For example, a temporary contract is usually not regarded as sufficient security for a mortgage; and it is bound to make those concerned wonder if they would have been better to choose another profession.

3.10   The Committee therefore recommends that the use of temporary contracts for fully qualified teachers should be strictly limited to circumstances where a period of absence is being covered, or where for specific reasons the position being filled is not likely to continue.

Continuing professional development (CPD)

3.11   The need for continuing development of knowledge and skills is well recognised in the education sector. The rapid changes that have taken place in many subjects; changes to the curriculum and teaching methods; developments in technology, particularly information and communications technology; and the constantly evolving role of schools in our society, all mean that a teacher's competences and knowledge need frequently to be reviewed and updated.

3.12   The Committee found that teachers were fully aware of the importance of CPD, and recognised that appropriate training could enhance their standing both within the profession and outside. At present most teachers fulfil their basic requirements for CPD by taking advantage of the five days each year designated for in-service training, time allocated within the existing framework for planned activities and sometimes "twilight courses" run by schools or local authorities: but attendance at courses under present arrangements also frequently necessitates absence during the teaching day, disrupting pupils' education and greatly adding to the need for supply cover, with all the problems that may bring. The Committee also found that there was widespread criticism of the quality of CPD on offer. Often courses did not provide what teachers required; many were thought to be disappointing, and to offer little value.

3.13   The Committee thinks that the present five designated days are quite inadequate to provide the amount and quality of CPD required; and believes that, given the long school holidays - a much longer break than that available to any other profession - many teachers would be prepared to give more of their time for this purpose outside normal pupil teaching hours, as long as it was seen to benefit their careers. But clearly no teacher can be expected to set aside time which would otherwise be spent at leisure, or just recuperating from the stresses and strains involved in teaching, unless appropriate high-quality CPD provision is available. In this context, it should be emphasised that

CPD can take a variety of forms, and is not by any means limited to centrally-organised, collective training courses. It may often involve individual modules or own-initiative activities, in some cases delivered by means of new information and communication technology.

3.14 The Committee is aware that the Scottish Executive is currently seeking to develop a national framework for CPD involving the establishment of a number of standards for teachers at key stages of their careers, and the identification of new methods of delivering the appropriate CPD to achieve them. The Committee welcomes this development, which it considers long overdue; and emphasises the key importance of adequate provision right across Scotland.

3.15 *The Committee recommends:*

- *That courses offered under the heading of CPD should be accredited at national level to ensure their quality and relevance;*

- *That local authorities should review their arrangements for the provision of organised CPD activity in their area to assess its effectiveness;*

- *That the Scottish Executive should establish a national register of approved CPD providers, and review the financing available to schools to support CPD activity;*

- *That every teacher should have an individual CPD plan agreed once a year with his or her immediate manager;*

- *And that all large primary and secondary schools which have not yet done so should designate a CPD co-ordinator from among the teaching staff to facilitate the management of CPD in the school. For smaller schools, a co-ordinator could be designated for each cluster.*

3.16 *In view of the importance of CPD, the Committee also recommends that, in consultation with the teaching unions, local authorities increase the time available for professional development by the equivalent of a further five days a year. This may be undertaken flexibly either outwith the school day or outside the pupil year. This additional commitment should be reflected in the salary structure.*

Sabbaticals

3.17 A number of teachers raised with the Committee the question of sabbaticals. The Committee considers that the opportunity for a term's break, say once in every ten years of a teacher's career, could - if used for well-focused research or other professional development - be of great value, not only in updating skills but in providing much needed refreshment in the course of what can be a stressful and at times repetitive career. Such breaks would have to be properly planned and organised, with the proposed activity on which time was to be spent approved by the Headteacher. But it could, for example, provide opportunity not only for a course leading to a qualification, but for language teachers to have experience in a school abroad, and for those in more technical subjects to update their knowledge outside the school environment.

3.18 To be workable, such breaks would have to be seen as an objective rather than as an entitlement. They would be expensive, because additional teaching resources would normally be required to cover them. Nevertheless, the Committee believes that sabbaticals could be valuable not only as a means of providing significant additional CPD and therefore as a way of improving the quality of the teaching force, but also in preventing later problems of burn-out that may necessitate early retirement. To this extent they may generate some offsetting saving. They should also be seen as the counterpart of our recommendation that TEI staff should spend more time in schools: exchanges between schools and TEIs could be a rewarding and self-financing element of any sabbatical scheme.

3.19 **The Committee therefore recommends that local authorities give early and positive consideration to establishing schemes of properly organised sabbaticals, which might be introduced on the basis of a term's break for every ten years spent teaching. It recognises, however, that such schemes would have considerable funding implications.**

Early retirement and "winding down"

3.20 It was put to the Committee that a number of teachers, by the time they reach their mid-fifties, are exhausted, and would wish to reduce their workload. Early retirement would be an attractive option to them, but only if their expected standard of living in retirement could be maintained. Some feel burnt-out; and to retain teachers in the profession in this condition is no service either to the profession or to the pupils whom they are required to teach. The measures to relieve workload recommended elsewhere in this report and more effective arrangements for CPD, particularly sabbaticals, should go some way towards reducing this problem. But with an average age in the profession of approximately 43, 50 per cent of teachers over the age of 45 and 20 per cent over 55, it has to be recognised that this may become an increasingly important issue over the years to come. It may also be better to allow some of those who wish to do so to leave the profession in the coming years than face a fairly massive exodus when the large numbers now in their late forties and early fifties reach the statutory retirement age in 15 to 20 years' time.

3.21 The general issue of reducing workload for older teachers can, however, be approached in a number of ways short of full retirement. A promoted teacher may feel he or she has spent long enough in management tasks and wish to return to classroom teaching for the last few years of a career. Older teachers might also be interested in giving up their full-time jobs but continuing on a part-time basis. Older and more experienced members of the profession have a major contribution to make in the area of mentoring and staff development. It would also be desirable for some older teachers to be able to transfer to supply work, perhaps on a part-time basis, rather than the present regrettable use for this purpose of new entrants (a practice on which we comment above).

3.22 At present it is difficult for those in their fifties to give up a promoted post for classroom teaching or to move to a part-time contract without this adversely affecting their pension to a significant extent. In part this has to do with pensions being based on final salary, but even where this problem can be avoided there remains the difficulty of topping-up pension contributions to the level of a full time or more senior post. Teachers' pensions are provided by the taxpayer, but on the basis of a 'notional fund' which is managed so as to be self-financing from teachers' and employers' contributions. The current estimated long-term contribution rate for the full benefits is 19 per cent, of which teachers contribute 6 per cent, to give a pension that amounts to half the final salary at the end of 40 years in employment, plus a lump sum of one and a half times the relevant salary, and spouse's benefits.

3.23 The Committee understands that the Scottish Public Pensions Agency has identified a new approach, based on reducing hours worked, to allow for part-time service, which would protect pensions to the extent that they would continue to be based on the final full-time salary. Teachers could make further contributions to the scheme during their part-time spell to top up their eventual entitlement. This option is thought to be broadly cost-neutral for the notional pension fund as a whole. A further cost-neutral approach, already adopted in England and Wales, involves the use of actuarially-reduced pensions to introduce new flexibilities for both teachers and employers. The Committee also notes that the recent Inland Revenue proposals to allow pensions to be drawn while members of the pension scheme are still working could lead to further useful options.

3.24   The Committee recognises that anything which goes beyond the schemes of this kind and requires an additional claim on public funding could be extremely expensive. Nevertheless, as well as relieving the obvious problem of teachers suffering from burn-out, the Committee considers that for the reasons outlined above more flexible arrangements that would permit moving to an unpromoted post or part-time work, as well as a carefully phased and discretionary one-off scheme of early retirement, could offer several advantages and at the same time help to bring some much-needed new blood into the profession.

3.25   *The Committee therefore recommends that the pension scheme and schemes for early retirement should be further investigated with the aim of achieving some of these benefits. The government should also consider a one-off early retirement scheme. Such a scheme could only run successfully if the government is able to provide additional funds, as has been done for other professions in the public sector. Options for "winding down" could, however, make a significant contribution towards improving the provision of supply cover and staff development activity in Scottish schools.*

3.26   *For the longer term, however, the teaching profession is aware that early retirement costs money, and it may be that the possibility of making larger contributions to the notional fund as a means of paying for an entitlement to retirement in advance of the statutory retirement age would find support. Higher contributions are paid by some other public sector employees who retire earlier than teachers. The Committee recommends that this should be discussed with the teachers' unions.*

SUPPORT

The contribution of support staff

3.27   If the best use is to be made of the teaching resource, it is essential for teachers to concentrate their main effort on teaching and other teaching related tasks, such as curriculum development, which they alone can do. It is a commonplace amongst teachers that the burdens of administration have grown and that a range of activities extending from financial management, care of the buildings and information technology equipment to the tasks associated with social inclusion are taking up more and more of their time. Linked to this are complaints that it is impossible to achieve promotion in the profession without getting involved in administration, and demands for a career structure to make it possible for teachers to gain increased reward and recognition while still staying in the classroom. It is certainly ironic if teachers, once they become senior, spend less and less of their time on the job for which they have been trained and more and more on tasks for which they have not been trained. It is equally odd to be promoted for professional competence but then to spend a greater part of one's time on non-professional work.

3.28   The Committee thinks that there are difficulties in any approach which seeks systematically to separate classroom teaching and learning and school management by means of a "twin-track" career structure right up through the professional grades: but in Section 4 of this report we make significant new proposals to reward maingrade teachers for excellence in, and commitment to, classroom teaching; and to enable them to achieve improved status within the profession while remaining in the classroom. In addition, we are strongly of the view that senior members of the profession should spend more of their time on teaching or education-related activities; and to this end we would like to see much greater use made of support at virtually all levels.

3.29   At the outset a distinction needs to be drawn between management of the profession, including responsibility and administrative matters closely related to teaching and education that require a teacher's expertise; and tasks for which a teacher is not specially equipped, and may even be less fitted than someone with a different training. The first category is common to senior personnel in most professions, and it is appropriate for senior members of the teaching staff in a school to undertake them. The second is not; and it is here that the scope lies for freeing up teachers' time, reducing the stress of the job and making the senior ranks of the profession more attractive to those who want to remain primarily teachers.

Senior staff

3.30   Among the written submissions to the Committee was the suggestion that the head of a school need not necessarily be trained as a teacher, and that in some respects a management background might be more appropriate. The Committee rejects this view. It believes that it is essential for all schools to be led by a head who has a background as a teacher. Only an experienced teacher can carry credibility with teaching colleagues, understand their concerns and those of parents. The management of a school raises quite different concerns from the management of a business, and only someone with experience of working in schools can be expected to have the right background and expertise. Nevertheless, Headteachers do need appropriate management training if they are to fulfil their functions to the necessary standard: the Committee expects the introduction of the Scottish Qualification for Headship to make a significant contribution in this respect.

3.31   In many schools it is unlikely that the Headteacher will be directly involved in significant amounts of classroom teaching: but all Headteachers should be involved extensively in leadership and management of learning and teaching and curriculum development in their schools, and in quality assurance of the education provision there. In order to free Headteachers and other senior staff to spend time in these ways, the Committee believes that all schools should have access to a Senior Administrative Officer (SAO) or "bursar" of equivalent standing to other senior teaching staff in the school and paid accordingly. This person would be responsible for the accounts and all financial matters related to the school, for matters relating to the maintenance of the building, for supplies and for school transport, and would have line management responsibility for all of the support staff in the school. Some schools have a person approximating to this role already, and the Committee met one in the course of its school visits: but, although it was a large secondary school, he had responsibility for other schools as well. The resource is therefore thinly spread at the present, where it exists at all, and for the majority of schools it is lacking altogether.

3.32   *The Committee therefore recommends that all schools of over 500 pupils should have a Senior Administrative Officer reporting to the headteacher at comparable level to senior teaching staff in the school. In the case of smaller schools, a Senior Administrative Officer should be given responsibility for a cluster of schools.*

3.33   Persons suitable for such a position may come from a variety of backgrounds. They could, for example, be people who have followed a career such as banking or accountancy, or may come from some other branch of the public sector; and it may be in some instances that a teacher, who feels in need of a change and does not wish to continue teaching, would wish to train up to take on this role. This has its parallel in the health service, where clinicians not infrequently decide to move into senior management. But there should be no pressure on teachers to take on this role; where it is done it should be the consequence of personal choice by the individual concerned.

3.34 The appointment of SAOs would be intended to make it possible for the senior teaching staff to spend more time on teaching and teaching-related activities. The Committee believes that should serve to make the senior grades of the profession more attractive to those who wish to go on being involved in teaching as a central activity; and should in turn have a positive effect on school performance.

3.35 The Committee is aware that in very small schools, particularly small rural primaries and nursery schools, the situation of the Headteacher is rather different. Most Headteachers in such schools will still have significant teaching commitments, with relief for management duties which varies across Scotland. The Committee has some reservations about this practice in terms of the availability of the Headteacher to deal with a wide variety of management issues which may arise, including health and safety matters. The assistance provided by SAOs should make a real difference in these small schools.

3.36 As far as the provision of management capacity in general is concerned, the Committee notes that the Scottish Executive is currently consulting on matters relating to school staffing in its review of the Schools (Scotland) Code 1956. *In this context, the Committee recommends that the amount of management time available to Headteachers and senior staff should be reviewed.*

3.37 Many of those who responded to the Committee's consultation document made reference to the approaches to reducing the burden of administrative work in schools outlined in the HMI/Accounts Commission publication "Time for Teaching". These included reviewing how routine or recurring tasks were carried out and streamlining them; increasing the use of information and communications technology and using it differently; and transferring some tasks to support staff. *The Committee has studied that report; endorses its main recommendations; and would wish to see all those involved give immediate attention to how best to put them into practice.*

Clerical staff

3.38 In a number of schools visited by the Committee, the devotion and diligence of clerical staff, particularly the school secretary, was crucial to the proper functioning of the school. This seemed to be a heavy responsibility to lay on what was sometimes only one individual who was not at a senior level; and in some schools in the primary sector, where the secretary is part-time, a lot of work which could be done by someone else was inevitably left to the Headteacher. If the Headteacher also spent considerable time in the classroom this could mean that at times there was no one to answer the telephone to deal with queries from parents or others who might need as a matter of urgency to contact the school. In cases where a child fell ill and parents were hard to contact, there could also be considerable problems and, indeed, risks. The appointment of SAOs will generally do much to strengthen the support from office-based staff, but this will apply less in small primary schools where the SAO may be responsible for a cluster. *The Committee therefore recommends that there should always be at least one member of staff in each school able to deal with routine emergencies and contact parents during the pupil day.*

Social inclusion

3.39   An area of growing importance is the amount of work associated with the Government's social inclusion policy. Teachers understand the importance of social inclusion and the part that education must play, if that policy is to be a success; and they have responded positively to that challenge. This can be seen in the way they have taken forward the New Community Schools initiative. Teachers in the special educational needs sector have particularly valuable experience to share in the context of inclusion. But many teachers who responded to the consultation document were concerned at the additional work which is involved in developing the social inclusion agenda. They also felt that there had been insufficient additional resources provided to accompany the new policy approach.

3.40   *The Committee considers it important that where increased demands arise from the social inclusion policy, these should be adequately resourced. This may have implications for staffing levels in schools. The Committee recommends that where the tasks involved do not require teachers' expertise and are more appropriate to other professionals, such as social and health workers and therapists, such professionals should be made available. Teachers will play their part: but it is not reasonable to add to the burdens of that profession by imposing tasks for which others are better fitted. It should also be underlined that parents, too, have an important part to play in supporting the work of the school. The removal of any doubt about the government's understanding of the implications of these matters would do much to reassure the teaching profession.*

3.41   In the course of the Committee's school visits, teachers reported a growing problem of indiscipline, which was a significant source of stress and overwork for teachers. This problem varied greatly from one school to another, and was in general more evident in urban areas than in small rural communities. The Committee believes that its recommendations elsewhere in this section should help considerably to reduce teachers' workload. *However, we also consider that effective action to tackle the problem of pupil indiscipline is essential not only to reduce the stress on teachers, but also in the interests of the majority of pupils for whom behaviour is not a problem. Teachers, parents, local authorities and the Executive all have a role to play; and the Committee recommends that the Executive carry out an appraisal of its policies in this regard, particularly the resources allocated to them.*

Information technology

3.42   The rapid development of information technology requires a special expertise and therefore staff with the appropriate skills. But it also offers significant benefits for teaching, as for many other professions. Teachers, like other professionals, are rapidly coming to terms with this, and many of them have either attended courses or are self-trained. The training possibilities offered through the New Opportunities Fund in the context of the government's policy for a National Grid for Learning are making a positive contribution in this respect. But not all teachers, even if they have been trained, will be expert, and lack of sufficient expertise can result in problems taking a long time to be solved if something goes wrong. *The Committee therefore recommends that every school or cluster of schools should have ready access to fully-trained personnel with the appropriate technical expertise and knowledge of the application of technology in the educational context.*

Supply cover

3.43   One issue that was frequently raised with the Committee in the course of its school visits was the difficulty experienced in securing appropriate supply cover to deal with planned or unplanned absences among the permanent teaching staff. The Committee surveyed local authorities on their use of supply staff. Their responses painted a very mixed picture of the situation, and indeed some authorities were unable to supply any information at all: but a significant number of authorities reported problems in obtaining supply teachers. The Committee's recommendations on the organisation of CPD should tend to reduce the demand for supply cover in relation to training and development activities; and our suggestions in relation to "winding down" should increase the potential pool of experienced supply staff available to authorities. *In addition, however, the Committee recommends that the Scottish Executive and local authorities review the way that supply cover is provided and managed across Scotland, and consider how it might be improved, for example by the constitution of standing teams of permanent peripatetic teachers.*

Classroom assistants and other para-professionals

3.44   In the course of its school visits the Committee met a large number of support staff, including classroom assistants in the primary sector. It is clear from evidence provided to the Committee, and from its discussions with those involved, that this development has been a considerable success and has helped significantly to reduce teacher workload. Some respondents to our consultation document suggested that classroom assistants could also have a role to play in the secondary sector. In particular, it was considered that art and design, home economics and ICT could all benefit from such assistance in the same way as has been provided for some time in science and technical education.

3.45   The Committee notes that around 1,500[1] classroom assistants are currently in place; and that the Scottish Executive has set a target that there should be a total of 5,000 classroom assistants in the primary sector by the end of the school year 2001/2002. However, it believes that there is much greater scope for the use of para-professionals to assist teachers and enable them to make the most productive use of their time. *It therefore recommends that the number of trained classroom assistants in the primary sector be increased substantially beyond the current target, with the objective that there should be at least one classroom assistant for every three primary classes in Scotland. In the secondary sector, a similar cadre of trained para-professionals should be provided, particularly in S1 and S2 and in appropriate subject areas, to help with the preparation of materials and any other tasks which will enable teachers to concentrate on their teaching duties.* Their introduction and the definition of their roles should be informed by the results of a number of pilot schemes across the country. Classroom assistants and other para-professionals may also have a role to play in areas such as health and safety and action to prevent bullying.

3.46   However, if the full potential of this initiative is to be realised, it is essential that such staff should receive appropriate training. In this context, the Committee welcomes the fact that the Scottish Executive is currently taking forward proposals on training programmes for classroom assistants in conjunction with the Scottish Qualifications Agency and the national training organisations.

Conclusion

3.47   The recommendations in this section would, in the Committee's view, do much to assist teachers to develop and maintain their expertise, to give new entrants a good start in the profession, to avoid problems of burn-out for older teachers, and to bring more

---

[1]   Full-time equivalents

young people into the profession. The Committee attaches great importance to its recommendations on support staff; and believes that they can make a significant contribution to reducing the workload and stress currently experienced by many teachers.

3.48　　The Committee recognises that these recommendations will cost money to implement. However, we wish to underline that they will deliver real gains for the education service as a whole. By freeing Headteachers, senior management teams and teachers to focus on tasks directly related to the process of teaching, there should also be real savings generated; while by improving initial training, arrangements for induction to the profession and access to high-quality CPD, and providing additional classroom support, there will be real benefits for teachers and a significant improvement in the quality of teaching and learning in all of our schools.

Section 4:
Career structure

4.1 An appropriate promotion and management structure in schools is an essential element of a successful education system. It exists to provide strategic direction and effective support for the central process of teaching and learning in the classroom. Effective organisation and leadership can make a real difference to the work of classroom teachers, and hence to the learning experience of children. Its importance in this respect should not be underestimated. However, promotion and management structures also fulfil other important functions: that of providing appropriate opportunities for career advancement for teachers; and, in conjunction with the pay structures accompanying them, that of encouraging, recognising and rewarding individual teachers' own contributions to the teaching and learning process. The Committee has therefore looked very closely at the existing promotion and management structures in Scottish schools.

Current structure

4.2 The Committee was struck by the complexity of the current structure in secondary schools, where there may be as many as seven grades of teacher: Headteacher, Depute Headteacher, Assistant Headteacher, Principal Teacher, Assistant Principal Teacher, Senior Teacher, and unpromoted teacher. This structure, which has developed over several decades, seemed to us to be overly hierarchical; and the differences in terms of function and weight or "size" of jobs of differing grades within the hierarchy were not always immediately clear to us. It was also noticeable that the difference in salaries these jobs attracted was often quite small. This seemed to us to raise a number of important questions about the rationale for the current system: whether it represents the appropriate structure of reward for the teaching profession; and whether it possesses the necessary flexibility to cope with the continually changing nature of education and consequent demands on the education service.

4.3 In the primary sector the position appears quite different. There are no Principal Teachers or Assistant Principal Teachers in primaries, and in many small schools there is no management "layer" between the Headteacher and a Senior or unpromoted teacher. This may be justified in the case of very small schools, but in the Committee's view seems far less so in larger primaries. It raises some important questions about management capacity in the primary sector, particularly where the Headteacher has a significant teaching load. These are, in part, addressed by our recommendations in the preceding section: but they are also relevant to the promotion and management structure.

Responses to the consultation exercise

4.4 Many of the respondents to the Committee's consultation document, and in particular the employers, Directors of Education and teaching unions, argued that the current promotion and management structure was excessively complicated and much too rigid. Some of them proposed an alternative structure involving three main grades: teacher, middle manager and senior manager (including Headteacher). Both the employers and some of the teaching unions suggested that the middle and senior management grades should be flexible, and that salaries should be determined by a process of job evaluation to be carried out at local level, on the basis of agreed criteria relating to the weight of job.

4.5   By contrast, the views of individual teachers in their submissions were less clear-cut. Some felt that the present structure adequately reflected the reality of day-to-day management in Scottish schools: more did not. A large number said that the post of Principal Teacher as subject head had played a crucial part in delivering successful curriculum development in the secondary sector, especially in relation to recent initiatives such as Higher Still: on the other hand, many pointed to the disparity in weight between Principal Teacher jobs in different subjects, which is not reflected in the salaries paid to them. Many people felt that the grade of Senior Teacher, of which a limited number had been introduced following the Main Review in 1986, had not achieved its objectives. They thought that its function was no longer clear, being neither a genuine management post nor an appropriate way of recognising and rewarding excellence in classroom teaching, because there were only a limited number of posts and because the additional salary by comparison with classroom teachers was very small. Some people thought that the function of the grade should be reviewed, while others said that it should be abandoned entirely.

4.6   The strongest message to emerge from the consultation exercise, however, from individuals and organisations alike, was a twofold one:

- that the only way for individual teachers to seek career and salary progression was to apply for management posts which would ultimately take them further away from the activity which had attracted them into the profession - classroom teaching - and into administrative and management activities, for which they might have neither the qualifications nor the inclination. There was no career track for teachers who wanted to stay in the classroom: the prospects for teachers who did not want to seek management responsibility were very poor. They quickly became stuck at the maximum salary for an unpromoted teacher, possibly for as long as thirty years;

- and that, in some situations, promotion possibilities were in any case too few and far between, mainly because they often depended on the departure or retirement of current postholders, and turnover was not great.

4.7   The Committee finds this a most unsatisfactory state of affairs. It considers that the career structure for the teaching profession must provide adequate opportunities for advancement for those teachers who do not wish to seek management posts, but to remain primarily in the classroom, practising and developing their expertise in teaching and learning. There should be a career pathway within the teaching profession which recognises and rewards the achievement of excellence in classroom teaching, without requiring a move into school management. We make specific recommendations on this issue later in this section.

Job evaluation exercise

4.8   The Committee commissioned PricewaterhouseCoopers to carry out an extensive research project to evaluate and compare a broad range of teaching jobs in Scotland; and to examine the salaries they attract with those paid in other occupations throughout Scotland and the UK requiring similar sets of skills and competences. This had two parts. The first involved an evaluation of a representative sample of teaching posts in different schools across Scotland, based on a wide-ranging and intensive programme of interviews with individual teachers and consultation meetings with groups. The purpose was to gain a clear and accurate picture of the skills and competences required for different jobs in the profession, and how they differed according to the different grades in the current structure. The second stage of the project, a comparative pay levels check, sought to compare the salaries these teaching posts attract with a range of other occupations requiring similar skills and competences. The project is described in Appendix C to this report; the findings in relation to pay are described in the following chapter.

4.9 The job evaluation exercise carried out for the Committee by PricewaterhouseCoopers suggested that, notwithstanding the wide variety of schools in Scotland and the range of different jobs within the profession according to sector, size of school and subject, teaching jobs fell into four basic categories:

> classroom teachers – including most Senior Teachers and Assistant Principal Teachers;

> Principal Teachers - including, in practice, some Assistant Principal Teachers;

> senior managers - including Assistant Headteachers and Depute Headteachers;

> Headteachers.

There were inevitably some differences in size between the various jobs examined, but the similarities in the levels of particular skills and competences required for the posts falling within these four broad bands was very marked, even when the relative weight attached to the different skills and competences was varied in order to test the robustness of the results.

Recommendations

4.10 On balance, the Committee considers that the current promotion and management structure no longer serves the teaching profession well. The Committee sees considerable advantage in a simpler structure, in terms of flexibility, transparency and enhanced reward prospects for individuals. *Having critically examined the findings by PricewaterhouseCoopers, it therefore recommends moving to a four-band structure as soon as practicable. This should have the following elements:*

- *A new enlarged main grade for classroom teachers, to incorporate all existing unpromoted teachers and Senior Teachers. In general, existing Assistant Principal Teachers would fall into this grade: but in some cases, where their posts carry significant management responsibilities, they might be assimilated into the middle management grade.* Within the new main grade there should be significantly improved prospects for reward and recognition for all existing classroom teachers, Senior Teachers and Assistant Principal Teachers, recognising their collegiate responsibility without the need to move into a management post. We make specific recommendations in this area below.

- *A middle management grade. The Committee recognises the key role played by Principal Teachers and recommends that the grade should continue. This grade would encompass all existing Principal Teachers and probably a limited number of Assistant Principal Teachers.* This grade would be mainly responsible for subject and guidance leadership within the secondary sector, as at present: but it should also be possible for Principal Teacher posts to be deployed more flexibly. For example, the Committee does not consider that every subject department should necessarily have a Principal Teacher – for small departments, a faculty approach might be more desirable. In other cases, schools may benefit from having Principal Teachers with broader thematic or whole-school responsibilities, such as support for learning or enterprise education. *It should also be possible to deploy Principal Teacher posts in the primary sector, as one way of addressing the need for more management capacity.* The Committee considers that these choices should be made at local level, in the light of local needs.

- *A single senior management grade, to be called Depute Headteacher, encompassing existing Assistant Headteachers and Depute Headteachers.* The Committee considers that the creation of a single grade would reflect the essentially collegiate nature of the job of a senior management team. It does not consider that the function of deputising for the Headteacher in the event of his or her illness or temporary absence, essential though it undoubtedly is, justifies a separate grade. Such a duty could more appropriately be shared between members of the senior management team. *Where a school is too small to justify a Depute Headteacher, another member of staff should be designated to deputise in the Headteacher's absence, and should be paid an allowance for doing so.* We make a recommendation on this in the following section.

  We would expect to see posts at this grade being deployed across a wide range of schools, in the primary sector as well as the secondary. We make proposals in the next section of this report on the salary such posts might attract with this consideration in mind.

- *A Headteacher grade.* The Committee considers that the job of Headteacher, with the significant representational and leadership functions and accountability it carries in all sizes of school, should be considered as a separate band within the profession.

4.11 *The Committee has recommended in the preceding section that the post of Senior Administrative Officer should be created to provide senior-level managerial support to schools in relation to non-teaching issues such as finance, buildings, purchasing and personnel. He or she should be considered as one of the senior management team alongside the Depute Headteachers, and should have responsibility beneath the Headteacher for the management of support staff in the school.*

4.12 *In order to recognise and reward excellence in the classroom and encourage continuing professional development within the teaching profession, the Committee also recommends that the Scottish Executive, together with the GTC and TEIs, and consulting local authority employers and the teaching unions, should develop by the end of this year a national programme and standards for Chartered Teacher status to be implemented by 1 April 2002. This programme should be open to all experienced classroom teachers. The Committee expects Chartered Teacher status to be within the reach of a significant majority of teachers; and anticipates that they would be motivated to achieve it. It would constitute a personal achievement, rather than a post. The programme should involve attestation through the annual review process[1] of high standards of teaching and professionalism, subject to external moderation to ensure consistent application across Scotland; it would require completion of a challenging and structured programme of relevant and accredited CPD, over a period of four years, aimed at improving teaching and other professional skills. In the early years of the scheme, consideration should be given to the practicality of a fast-track procedure for teachers already at the top of the scale and who have already undertaken significant amounts of CPD, subject to validation.*

---

[1] We make specific recommendations on
    review procedures in Section 7 of this report

4.13   *Progress towards, and achievement of, Chartered Teacher status would be rewarded with additional salary points. Once acquired, teachers would keep the status and the associated salary points if they transferred to another school. Acquisition of Chartered Teacher status would not involve taking on any additional management responsibility beyond that of a maingrade teacher. We would, however, expect that Chartered Teachers would play an important part as role models for junior colleagues. In the Committee's view, such a chartering scheme should provide an attractive option for teachers who do not wish to seek promotion to middle management but to develop their classroom skills through CPD.*

4.14   *Furthermore, the Committee recommends the introduction, on the same timescale, of a more demanding programme for Advanced Chartered Teacher status for which all Chartered Teachers would be able to apply. It would involve a programme of CPD focusing on development of classroom practice through research and advanced learning, in conjunction with the TEIs. Achievement of Advanced Chartered Teacher status would be subject to external assessment of classroom expertise. As for the Chartered Teacher, progress towards, and achievement of, Advanced Chartered Teacher status would attract additional salary; Advanced Chartered Teachers could earn as much as or more than Principal Teachers.*

4.15   *Although ACT status is intended to be an end in itself for the dedicated and experienced teacher who wishes to develop his or her career in the classroom, Advanced Chartered Teachers would be expected to make a wide contribution towards the development of teaching and learning in their own schools and beyond, with particular emphasis on training and mentoring of junior colleagues. They would ultimately become a resource for the nation in driving forward national educational standards.*

4.16   Our proposals are outlined more fully in the following annex; our salary proposals are discussed in the next section.

CHARTERED AND ADVANCED CHARTERED TEACHERS

Chartered Teacher programme

1. The aim of our proposal for a Chartered Teacher programme is to provide an alternative route for experienced classroom teachers who wish to develop their professional expertise within the classroom, rather than seeking promotion to a management post. Although the standard will be challenging, we expect Chartered Teacher status to be within the reach of a significant majority of teachers. We anticipate that teachers will be motivated to achieve it.

2. When the maximum point in the maingrade scale has been reached, and the objectives of the annual review cycle have been successfully completed, the experienced teacher will be able to choose whether he or she wishes to participate in the four-year programme leading to Chartered Teacher status.

3. The Charter programme will include:

    (a) An agreed programme of accredited CPD targeted to the individual's development needs;

    (b) Attestation, through the annual review process, of high standards of teaching and professionalism

    Implementation of the scheme will need to be subject to external moderation to ensure comparable standards across the country.

    Progress through the programme will be dependent on successful completion of the relevant CPD and attainment of the personal objectives set at the annual review. It will be recognised by the award of additional salary points. Completion of the whole programme will lead to the formal award by the GTC of Chartered Teacher status: a personal achievement, not an appointment to a post. The Chartered Teacher will not be expected to take on any additional management responsibility beyond that of a maingrade teacher. We would, however, expect that Chartered Teachers would play an important part as role models for junior colleagues. Chartered Teacher status, and the salary point associated with it, should follow the teacher if he or she transfers to another post.

Advanced Chartered Teacher programme

5. A Chartered Teacher intending to embark on the four year journey to Advanced Chartered status will identify, in conjunction with the senior management of their school and TEIs, a rigorous programme of continuing professional development which will involve further development of classroom practice through research and advanced learning. Teachers embarking on the programme will contribute a significant commitment of their own time and resources to its successful completion.

6. The Advanced Chartered Teacher programme will comprise:

    (a) advanced learning - successful completion of a set of advanced courses on the themes of child learning and support;

    (b) completion of a research project based on teaching and learning;

(c) broadened experience through a work placement in another educational institution or social work or health institution;

(d) evidence of the application and dissemination of the results of learning and research.

7. TEIs and other providers will require to develop courses and modules that will underpin the Advanced Chartered Teacher programme. It is expected that developments in ICT will support the programme in general, and in particular will facilitate access to parts (a) and (b) of the above programme for teachers living in all parts of Scotland.

8. Chartered Teachers will progress to the next year of the ACT programme on successful completion of their targets as assessed at their annual review and have their salary adjusted accordingly. This annual assessment will involve input from an external body, such as a TEI, which will monitor the Chartered Teacher's progress and provide the essential element of moderation of standards across schools.

9. The Scottish Executive, GTC and TEIs will jointly develop criteria for distinguishing exceptional classroom teaching skills and have an overview of the CPD required for the Advanced Chartered Teacher programme. Those wishing to follow the Advanced Chartered Teacher programme will register with the GTC, which will record progress and play a part in confirming the teacher's status on the programme and associated level of pay should the teacher transfer to another school.

10. Teachers achieving Advanced Chartered status will be expected to play a significant role in promoting standards of excellence in teaching. The focus of the ACT programme is the delivery of high-quality classroom practice identified through action-oriented research and the implementation of teaching practices and methods that enhance the education of pupils. Consequently, Advanced Chartered Teachers will become a resource for the nation as well as for their schools and local authorities.

11. Although Chartered Teacher status is intended to be an end in itself for the dedicated teacher who wishes to develop a career in the classroom, it will be possible for Chartered Teachers to move into other leadership roles. The GTC, TEIs and local authorities will require to develop CPD pathways which will provide the necessary training for Chartered and Advanced Chartered Teachers who aspire to posts in the management grades.

12. Local authorities will have responsibility, in conjunction with the Scottish Executive, for ensuring that secure and ongoing resources are made available to schools to support the agreed CPD activities of the Chartered and Advanced Chartered Teacher programmes.

Section 5:
Pay

5.1 The success of the schools depends on the quality of the teachers who work in them. So if Scotland is to have a first-class education service for the 21st century, teachers' salaries must be set at a level to recruit, retain and motivate high-quality graduates. The salary structure for the teaching profession must be designed to promote and reward effective teaching and management in schools; and it should complement the promotion and management structures within the profession.

5.2 With these objectives in mind, the Committee has examined trends in teachers' salaries over the past quarter of a century; the current level of teachers' salaries by comparison with those in other occupations; and the current situation in relation to recruitment, retention and motivation of teachers.

Trends in teachers' pay

5.3 A large number of the respondents to the Committee's consultation document, including the local authority employers and the main teaching unions, argued that teachers' salaries had not kept pace with those of other professions over recent years, and should therefore be reviewed. In its written evidence to the Committee, the EIS reported the salary settlements in each of the years since 1990. A comparison with the corresponding inflation rates reveals that in four years since 1993, teachers' pay awards were lower than inflation. Over the 1990s as a whole, however, the figures submitted by the EIS show that settlements had outstripped inflation. The EIS also argued that settlements awarded to teachers in Scotland had closely matched those awarded to English and Welsh teachers and local authority white-collar employees.

5.4 Data for annual pay settlements reveal only part of what has been happening to teachers' pay, however. Some teachers benefit from incremental progression up salary scales, others gain promotion. To capture these dimensions, those researching pay trends also use data on average earnings. A number of submissions to the Committee referred to the Average Earnings Index (AEI), pointing out that teachers' salaries had increased by less than this index over the 1990s.

5.5 Earnings data need to be interpreted with great care. Changes in earnings of any group of employees reflect changes in the composition of that group: for example, when the number of new recruits entering the profession outnumber those retiring, average earnings will tend to fall, because those who retire tend to earn more than new entrants.

5.6 However the AEI has also been the subject of much criticism in recent years; and for a short time towards the end of the 1990s it was officially suspended, pending reviews of its construction.

5.7 The EIS also submitted to the Committee a study of trends in teachers' earnings, based on the New Earnings Survey (NES), which it had commissioned from the University of Paisley. This study argued that over the period since the Main Review in 1986, the growth in teachers' earnings had been bettered by most manual workers in Scottish local authorities, by male nurses, and by male teachers in England and Wales. However, it also showed that for a few groups, particularly local authority non-manual staff, lower rises had been recorded.

5.8   The study concluded that teachers' earnings had fallen in real terms since 1993, declining by four percentage points. It suggested that, in order to restore their relative position in relation to non-manual workers as a whole immediately after the Main Review, male teachers' salaries would need to have been increased by 8% in 1999 and women teachers' salaries by 11.8%. It also argued that in order to restore teachers' salaries to the same level in comparison to some professions - doctors, solicitors and accountants - as they enjoyed at the beginning of the 1990s, substantial increases of up to £100 a week would be needed.

5.9   Neither the EIS, the other unions, nor the employers were prepared to take a position in their submissions to the Committee and their subsequent oral evidence on the amount by which they considered salaries should be increased in the light of these various developments.

5.10   The Committee commissioned its own study on trends in the earnings of teachers and other groups in Scotland over the period 1975 to 1999 from Professors Bell and Elias of the Universities of Stirling and Warwick. This study, which is reproduced as Appendix A, draws on the same statistics as those used by the University of Paisley, but also uses the raw data collected by the Office of National Statistics for the NES and made available to researchers in a few leading UK universities.

5.11   The figures underlying the study by Professors Bell and Elias are compatible with those in the University of Paisley study: but they cover a longer time period, and draw on a wider range of occupational groups for their comparisons. The study confirms the proposition that teachers' earnings have declined in real terms since 1993. (See graph below.) However, it also shows that the distribution of earnings in the economy as a whole has widened, and that within that distribution teachers have done better than the average. And it demonstrates that teachers' position relative to other groups differs according to the choice of comparator. For example, they have fared less well than solicitors but better than teachers in further or higher education. It should be noted that comparisons with solicitors, and with doctors and accountants, present particular problems, because (with the exception of hospital doctors) many in these groups are self-employed and therefore not easily compared with teachers.

Figure 1: Real weekly earnings in Scotland: teachers and others by gender - real (1998 prices)

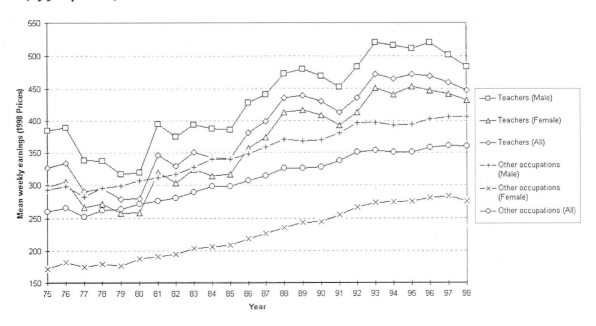

5.12   The Bell and Elias report also shows that the dispersion of earnings within the teaching profession has narrowed significantly over the period, whereas for nearly all other professions it has increased. This raises questions about whether the structure of teachers' salary scales is appropriate.

5.13   Overall, however, the study by Professors Bell and Elias does not show that there has been a clear and sustained decline in teachers' salaries in relation to all other comparable groups. In view of the widely held opinion that there had indeed been such a decline, the Committee was somewhat surprised by these findings: but it is firmly of the view that the Stirling/Warwick study is a reliable and balanced one.

5.14   One other message to emerge from the analysis of pay trends was the fact that over the past quarter of a century teachers' salaries have progressed in fits and starts, with a series of small increases, then a major upward revision – often following an independent review – then further small increases. The Committee considers this pattern to be unsatisfactory, and liable to lead to discontent. It attaches importance to finding a system which will ensure more orderly progression; and makes recommendations in this respect in Section 8 of this report.

Current salary levels

5.15   In order to assess how current salary levels for the teaching profession compare with those for other occupations requiring similar skills and competences, the Committee instructed PricewaterhouseCoopers (PwC) to carry out a pay levels check against a broad range of organisations from both public and private sectors in Scotland and England. This exercise, which is described in Appendix C of this report, involved matching a representative range of jobs within the teaching profession - at differing grades, in differing schools, covering different subject areas - with the nearest comparable jobs in other organisations, on the basis of detailed job descriptions analysing the skills and competences they required and comparing the total cash package they attracted.

5.16   This comparison involved organisations both in Scotland and in England, because the Committee is of the view that Scottish teachers operate in a UK-wide labour market; and that the competitiveness of Scottish teachers' salaries should therefore be judged in that context. PwC also looked at the total financial package available to employees in comparator organisations: but they did not take account in detail of non-cash benefits because they were difficult to evaluate precisely in cash terms, although in broad terms their value on average was taken as offsetting the much longer holidays available to teachers.

5.17   The main findings of the pay levels check were:

- that the salaries for classroom teachers are at the upper quartile[1] of the distribution of pay compared with the jobs of similar weight in the total sample of organisations surveyed;

- that their salaries are in fact some 10 per cent above the median[2] level for the public sector sample;

- these findings were influenced heavily by the fact that, like most classroom teachers (about 70 per cent), the teachers in posts examined in the exercise are at the top of the main salary scale;

---

[1]   The upper quartile is the value below which lie three-quarters of the sample surveyed

[2]   The median is the value in the middle of the sample surveyed

- that salaries at the bottom end of the Principal Teacher scale are comparable to the median for the organisations surveyed, and above the public sector median, but that they fall away from the median by about 5 per cent at the top end;

- that the salaries of Assistant Headteachers and Depute Headteachers fall below the market median by around 10 per cent and at the top end by where they approach the lower quartile,[3] by around 15 per cent;

- and that salaries for all Headteachers are below the median by about 15 per cent at the bottom end, rising to 20 per cent for the largest jobs, where they approach the level of the lower quartile.

- But that, compared to the public sector sample of the survey, Headteachers' salary levels are at the upper quartile.

5.18 Taken together, these two independent studies which we commissioned suggest that, apart from the decline since 1993, a generalised and substantial uplift of teachers' salaries to remedy a sustained period of erosion, or to reflect levels available elsewhere in today's marketplace, would not be fully justified: but they do suggest that adjustments are necessary, particularly towards the top end of the profession, if salaries are to remain competitive; and that the progression of teachers' salaries needs to be more stable. However, there are several other important factors at play which the Committee felt it important to consider before coming to an overall view.

Graduate salary levels

5.19 A number of respondents to the consultation document drew particular attention to the level of starting salary in the teaching profession, which is currently £14,877 for an honours graduate; and argued that this was too low by comparison with starting salaries on offer elsewhere, and was therefore unattractive to high-quality potential new entrants to the teaching profession. The EIS evidence to the Committee pointed to the findings of the Income Data Services (IDS) Management Pay Review for 1998/99, which estimated the average starting salary of a graduate at £17,360. The review of employers belonging to the Association of Graduate Recruiters (AGR) suggested that the average starting salary was around £17,500. According to the latest Graduate Market Trends Survey and Vacancy Survey, the average basic salary for graduates advertised in the year to August 1999 rose by 7.7% to £16,430. However, the most recent annual graduate survey carried out by Barclays Bank at the end of 1998 suggested an average starting salary of £13,400.

5.20 The difference between these surveys is likely to be due to the different average measures used: but the main reason why the Barclays survey is so much lower seems to be that it includes all graduates, even where they were in jobs for which graduate qualifications were not essential, whereas the AGR and IDS surveys only cover graduate entrants to the management training schemes of a limited number of "blue chip" employers. Taken together, the surveys do suggest that the current starting salary for teachers is low in relation to that for other occupations competing for graduates: but it is not possible to say with confidence by exactly how much. They also reveal that competition for high-quality graduates has intensified in recent years. The key question is to what extent the level of starting salary has an impact on recruitment of high-quality graduates into the teaching profession.

---

[3] The lower quartile is the value above which lie three-quarters of the sample surveyed

Recruitment to the teaching profession

5.21   In order to assess the current situation in relation to teacher recruitment, the Committee commissioned a wide range of statistical information from the Scottish Executive, the General Teaching Council and teacher education institutions. Some of this information is contained in Appendix F of this report. It also surveyed local authorities; and raised the issue with teachers and Headteachers in the course of its programme of school visits.

5.22   Recruitment to the teaching profession is managed by the individual local authorities: but the Scottish Executive and Scottish Higher Education Funding Council carry out an annual workforce planning exercise to estimate future requirements, and the number of places available for initial teacher education at the TEIs is established in the light of those estimates.

5.23   The statistics on applications to TEIs show a marked increase in applications in both the primary and secondary sectors over the 1990s; and the ratio of applications to places has steadily increased in the primary sector. In the secondary sector, applications per place rose significantly between 1990 and 1996, then decreased in the last two years, while still remaining significantly in excess of the places available: but were significantly less than primary. Analysis of the qualifications of entrants to teacher training suggests that trainees are more highly qualified than ever before. The numbers of graduates of TEIs has remained broadly constant over the last decade. Taken together, these figures do not suggest a general difficulty in attracting potential new teachers into initial training.

5.24   The TEIs, however, report a decline in applicants for secondary training, and difficulties in filling their quotas in a number of subject areas. They argue that the figures are not as healthy as they appear because they cover multiple applications and applications which potential trainees will only follow through if they are unsuccessful in pursuing another option. They also argue that the recent tightening of entry qualifications required for teacher training by the Scottish Executive had had the effect of reducing the number of eligible candidates, and reducing the number eligible to train in two secondary subjects rather than one. They therefore consider that very real problems of recruitment in the secondary sector are approaching.

5.25   This message was borne out during the Committee's school visits, and in many of the responses to its consultation document. Moreover, many of the local authorities responding to a Committee survey, reported difficulties in recruiting teachers for certain subject areas, particularly for promoted posts. In many cases vacancies had to be re-advertised, sometimes more than once, before they were filled. The Committee viewed these circumstances with concern, regarding it as vital that the education service is able to fill posts with candidates of suitably high quality.

Retention

5.26   The statistics provided by the Scottish Executive concerning the numbers of teachers leaving the profession over the past decade are reproduced at Appendix F. They suggest a steady decline in the total: but a significant number of those leaving the profession going to teaching outside Scotland. This may in part be due to domestic circumstances, or it may be a reflection of dissatisfaction with the profession in Scotland. A number of the teaching unions and individual respondents to the consultation document have suggested that there has been an increase in the number leaving the profession through ill health brought about by excessive workload and stress. This is not immediately apparent from the statistics: but it cannot be discounted. The recent proposals to enhance the pay of teachers south of the border will also create additional pressures to which the Committee believes it needs to respond.

Motivation

5.27 A large number of respondents to the consultation document reported extremely low morale in the teaching profession. Many attributed this to issues of workload: but the great majority argued that it was the result of a salary structure which neither rewarded teachers sufficiently for their hard work nor provided incentives for improvement. The Committee finds this situation very worrying.

Salary structure

5.28 The current salary structure for the Scottish teaching profession has a number of distinctive features, and includes a number of anomalies:

- the basic payscale for classroom teachers is relatively long, with nine points between the honours graduate starting salary and the top of the unpromoted scale;

- the size of increments on this scale is small;

- Senior Teachers and Assistant Principal Teachers are paid on the same short three-point scale which only extends £2,000 above the unpromoted scale;

- Principal Teachers are paid a six-point range exclusively on the basis of school roll. Assistant Headteachers, on the other hand, are paid on different points according to sector, but the same within each sector, regardless of school roll;

- Deputes and Headteachers are paid on different ranges according to sector, and according to school roll within each sector, whatever the similarity in their responsibilities between the different sectors might be;

- The senior management team in smaller primary schools are paid less than Principal Teachers in large secondaries, despite their significantly broader responsibilities.

5.29 Many of the respondents to the consultation document, including the employers and the main teaching unions, drew attention to the length of the basic scale. Many individual teachers emphasised their view that the top of the unpromoted scale was insufficient for a skilled and experienced teacher; and that it tended to drive him or her out of the classroom in search of an improved salary.

Recommendations

5.30 In the light of the above considerations, and of its recommendations on a new promotion and management structure for the teaching profession, the Committee considers that the teaching profession requires a new salary structure which:

- provides an appropriate and competitive incentive structure to recruit, retain and motivate high-quality graduates;

- is simple, transparent and flexible;

- creates, as far as possible, an integrated framework for the different sectors;

- removes the anomalies in the current system;

- promotes collegiality and mobility;

- and recognises and rewards excellence in the classroom.

5.31 *With these objectives in mind, the Committee makes the following specific recommendations:*

- *The starting salary for all graduate entrants should be increased to £17,000;*

- *Probationer teachers should receive an increase of £500 after their first year's service, and a further £1,500 on completion of the probationary period, so that the starting salary for a fully qualified main grade teacher is £19,000;*

- *The scale for maingrade teachers should proceed in five equal steps to a new increased maximum of £26,000 for a fully experienced teacher;*

- *Beyond that maximum, teachers embarking on the programme to acquire Chartered Teacher status described in the preceding section of this report should proceed by further annual increments of £750, (subject to satisfactory progress through the programme) to a salary for a certified Chartered Teacher of £29,000;*

- *Teachers wishing to proceed to Advanced Chartered Teacher status should receive further annual increments of £1,250 over the course of their four year programme to a salary for a certified Advanced Chartered Teacher of £34,000;*

- *Principal Teachers should be paid on a short, three-point range going from £30,000 to £35,000, with placement to depend on school roll;*

- *The new Depute Headteacher grade should be paid on a four-point range from £30,000 to £44,000, depending on school roll. In view of the collegiate nature of work in the senior management team within a school, Depute Headteachers within the same school should all receive the same salary;*

- *Headteachers should be paid on a nine-point range going from £36,000 to £61,500, depending on school roll.*

Revised salary scales are set out in Annex A to this section.

5.32 In reaching its decisions, the Committee has taken careful note of the fact that the employers and some of the teaching unions would favour a system of job evaluation to determine placement on salary scales at middle management level and above. We have thought carefully about this proposal, but we have rejected it, because we feel that carrying out a programme of job evaluation for all of the posts concerned would be a time-consuming, costly, cumbersome and potentially controversial process of uncertain outcome. For the purposes of transparency and simplicity, we have therefore based our proposed scales on the school roll, on the basis that size of school is a reasonable, objective and well-understood indicator of the likely weight of a job.

5.33 The calculations underlying the figures in the annex are based on existing salaries. Since future negotiations on pay will fall to the successor body to the SJNC, which we consider in Section 8 of this report, and since this will take some time to establish, for the sake of clarity we outline below our proposals for the timetable for future pay settlements:

- The Committee notes that the SJNC is currently discussing a cost-of-living increase to apply from 1 April 2000. **Any increase agreed should be added to our recommended scales**;

- Our proposed transition to the new scales should begin on 1 April 2001; and should replace pay negotiations for that year. In most cases, the scales we propose would be introduced on a staged basis, and would not become fully payable until 1 April 2002 or, in some cases, beyond;

- the successor body to the SJNC should begin its work with the normal pay review due from 1 April 2002.

Transition arrangements

5.34 The Committee's proposals for transition to the new scales are described in Annex B to this Section. The main elements are as follows:

- On 1 April 2001, all existing classroom teachers would receive a first increase of between 8 and 12 per cent, depending on their position on the current scale. They would then move to the appropriate point on the new scale on 1 April 2002, allowing for normal incremental progression in the intervening period;

- In 2001, all existing Senior Teachers and Assistant Principal Teachers would receive an increase of 8 per cent; in 2002, they would be assimilated to the penultimate point in the Chartered Teacher scale, allowing for incremental progression in the meantime. However, some APTs might be assimilated onto the new PT range, depending on the functions of their post;

- In 2001, all Principal Teachers would receive an increase of 8 per cent. They would move onto the appropriate point on the new range the following year;

- Existing Assistant Headteachers, Depute Headteachers and Headteachers would receive a flat rate increase of 8 per cent in 2001. They would then receive the second instalment needed to take them to the appropriate point on the new range in 2002.

- In any cases where the overall increase needed to reach the new point on the Depute or Headteacher range exceeds 15 per cent, however, the balance over the initial 8 per cent in 2001 would be staged over a further period.

Conservation of salary

5.35 Any teacher for whom the initial increase would take him or her beyond the appropriate point on the new ranges, or whose salary might fall as a direct result of the restructuring we propose, would still receive the initial increase in full, but would then have his or her salary conserved in cash terms until the appropriate salary on the new range overtakes it.

5.36 The Committee does not, however, consider that indefinite conservation can be justified in the longer term for further individual changes which may be needed. It notes that indefinite conservation is not the practice elsewhere, and finds it hard to see why teachers should be an exception. It therefore recommends that conservation arrangements for teachers be brought into line with those for other local authority employees, whose salaries may be conserved for a maximum of three years. Those currently on conserved salaries, however, should continue to be covered by the current arrangements.

Additional flexibility

5.37 The Committee considers that these new salary scales offer a significantly enhanced prospects for all the teachers; and should serve to promote and reward excellence in classroom teaching and in management in Scotland's schools. Taken together with the new simpler grade structure, they should also encourage the necessary flexibility to respond to changing pressures. However, the Committee also recognises that in some circumstances there maybe particular short-term needs which require to be addressed at middle management level, but which do not justify a permanent re-organisation of the middle management tier within a school. These might include the need to review the curriculum in a particular subject area. *In these circumstances, the Committee considers that Headteachers should have the flexibility to award additional payments of up to £1,000 on a time-limited basis to Principal or maingrade teachers in recognition of such additional tasks. The budgetary arrangements for schools should be made more flexible to allow Headteachers the discretion to do so. Any additional payments should not, however, be consolidated and should not normally exceed two years in duration.*

5.38 *In schools too small to justify a permanent Depute, the Headteacher should also have the flexibility to make an additional payment to another member of staff for deputising in his or her absence, without prejudice to the existing arrangements for "acting-up" during more prolonged absences.*

5.39 *Similarly, Headteachers should have the discretion to make modest additional payments to maingrade teachers for activities going above and beyond their normal responsibilities. These should not exceed the implied hourly rate of the individual teacher's salary; and should not be consolidated. Budgetary arrangements should be such as to allow Headteachers the flexibility to make such payments; the criteria for doing so should be agreed at local level, and should be made available to all staff.*

5.40 *More generally, within the context of arrangements for devolved school management it should be possible for Headteachers, in co-operation with the local authority, to vary the management structure and deployment of posts within a school in the light of changing circumstances. The Committee recommends that the Scottish Executive and local authorities examine current practice with a view to facilitating such flexibility.*

Conclusions

5.41 The Committee considers that these recommendations provide the basis for a new start for the teaching profession in Scotland. They recognise the need for salaries to be set at a competitive level; they promote and reward excellence in classroom teaching and in management in schools; they are simple and transparent and responsive to local needs; and they remove the main anomalies in the existing salary structure.

5.42 On average the Committee's proposal would represent an increase for existing classroom teachers of between 13.9 and 19.3 per cent over two years, in addition to normal incremental progression; for Senior Teachers and APTs of 13.5 per cent in addition to normal progression; for PTs of between 11.8 and 22.6 per cent; and for members of the senior management team of at least 8 per cent and in some cases significantly more, depending on the size of school.

5.43 The introduction of Chartered Teacher status offers maingrade teachers the possibility of an increase of 27.5 per cent over the existing maximum for classroom teachers in return for investment in improving their skills, and should offer a real incentive to remain in the classroom; while the introduction of Advanced Chartered Teacher status offers the prospect of very significant rewards, some 49 per cent above the current classroom teacher maximum, for those teachers who want to build on their classroom skills to make a real contribution to the wider life of the school and the Scottish education service as a whole.

5.44 The proposals for Depute Headteachers and Headteachers should serve to encourage the candidates to aspire to leadership positions within the profession, and should recognise the burden of responsibility laid on their shoulders.

5.45 And finally, the Committee's recommendations on additional flexibility payments should allow Headteachers to respond to changing demands, deploy resources creatively, and recognise and reward additional contributions to the school's objectives from maingrade and Principal Teachers over and above their normal duties.

New salary scales[1]

Maingrade teachers[2]

Existing Scale Points	Existing Scale (Effective from 01/04/99)	New Scale Points	New Scale (Effective from 01/04/02)
2	£14,877	1	£17,000
3	£15,558	2	£17,500
4	£16,245	3	£19,000
5	£17,103	4	£20,400
6	£18,126	5	£21,800
7	£19,152	6	£23,200
8	£20,265	7	£24,600
9	£21,546	8[3]	£26,000
10	£22,743	9	£26,750
		10	£27,500
		11	£28,250
		12[4]	£29,000
		13	£30,250
		14	£31,500
		15	£32,750
		16[5]	£34,000

(1)   The transition to the new scales will begin on 1 April 2001 (see Annex B)
(2)   The new scale should be uprated to reflect the outcome of the current negotiation in the SJNC on a cost-of-living increase to apply from 1 April 2000 (see paragraph 5.33 above)
(3)   Fully experienced maingrade teacher
(4)   Chartered Teacher
(5)   Advanced Chartered Teacher

Note   Under the new scale all graduates will be appointed at new scale point 1; therefore no equivalents have been shown in the new scale corresponding to old scale points 0 and 1.

Principal Teacher range[1]

School Roll Bands (Existing)	Existing salary	School Roll Bands (New)	New salary (Effective from 01/04/02)
Up to 300	£25,659	Up to 550	£30,000
301 – 600	£26,508	551 to 1050	£32,500
601 – 800	£27,372	Over 1050	£35,000
801 – 1000	£28,215		
1001 – 1300	£29,082		
Over 1300	£29,934		
Special Educational Needs	£25,998		£30,000

[1] The new range should be uprated to reflect the outcome of the current negotiation in the SJNC on a cost-of-living increase to apply from 1 April 2000 (see paragraph 5.33 above)

Depute Headteacher range[1]

School Roll Bands (Existing)	Existing salary	School Roll Bands (New)	New salary (Effective from 01/04/02)
1) Primary			
Up to 450	£28,848	Up to 150	£30,000
Up to 600	£29,523	151 to 550	£34,000
Over 600	£31,539	551 to 1050	£39,000
		Over 1050	£44,000
2) Secondary			
Up to 100	£32,886	Up to 150	£30,000
Up to 300	£33,567	151 to 550	£34,000
Up to 550	£34,377	551 to 1050	£39,000
Up to 800	£35,505	Over 1050	£44,000
Up to 1050	£36,618		
Up to 1300	£37,743		
Up to 1550	£38,862		
Over 1550	£39,987		
3) Special Educational Needs			
Up to 60	£29,523	Up to 60	£34,000
Up to 100	£30,870	61 to 100	£36,500
Up to 140	£31,539	Over 100	£39,000
Over 140	£32,211		

[1]   The new range should be uprated to reflect the outcome of the current negotiation in the SJNC on a cost-of-living increase to apply from 1 April 2000 (see paragraph 5.33 above)

Headteacher range[1]

School Roll Bands (Existing)	Existing salary	School Roll Bands (New)	New salary (Effective from 01/04/02)
1) Primary			
Up to 50	£28,848	Up to 50	£36,000
Up to 150	£30,870	51 to 150	£40,000
Up to 300	£32,211	151 to 300	£44,000
Up to 450	£33,567	301 to 550	£47,500
Up to 600	£36,618	551 to 800	£51,000
Over 600	£38,862	801 to1050	£54,000
		1051 to1300	£56,500
		1301 to1550	£59,000
		Over 1550	£61,500
2) Secondary			
Up to 100	£33,567		
Up to 300	£37,743		
Up to 550	£41,109		
Up to 800	£43,350		
Up to 1050	£46,716		
Up to 1300	£48,960		
Up to 1550	£51,198		
Over 1550	£53,439		
3) Special Educational Needs			
Up to 30	£30,870	Up to 30	£40,000
Up to 60	£32,886	31 to 60	£44,000
Up to 100	£34,377	61 to 100	£45,750
Up to 140	£36,618	101 to 140	£47,500
Over 140	£38,862	Over 140	£51,000

(1) The new range should be uprated to reflect the outcome of the current negotiation in the SJNC on a cost-of-living increase to apply from 1 April 2000 (see paragraph 5.33 above)

Transition to new salary scales[1]

Existing classroom teachers

Current salary	Salary on 01/08/00 after normal incremental progression	Transitional scale – 01/04/01	Increase in salary over point achieved by 01/08/00 (%)	Salary on 01/08/01 after normal incremental progression on transitional scale	New scale - 01/04/02	Increase in salary over point achieved by 01/08/01 (%)
£14,877	£15,558	£17,425	12	£17,870	£19,000*	6.3
£15,558	£16,245	£17,870	10	£18,813	£20,400	8.4
£16,245	£17,103	£18,813	10	£19,939	£21,800	9.3
£17,103	£18,126	£19,939	10	£20,684	£21,800	5.4
£18,126	£19,152	£20,684	8	£21,886	£23,200	6.0
£19,152	£20,265	£21,886	8	£23,270	£24,600	5.7
£20,265	£21,546	£23,270	8	£24,562	£26,000	5.9
£21,546	£22,743	£24,562	8	N/A	£26,000	5.9
£22,743	N/A	£24,562	8	N/A	£26,000	5.9

Notes Existing classroom teachers will move onto a transitional scale, involving increases of between 8 and 12 per cent (depending on current scale point) on 1 April 2001. They will receive their increments on 1 August 2000 and 1 August 2001; and will move, with a further uplift, onto the new maingrade teacher scale on 1 April 2002. Placement on the new scale will allow existing teachers to reach the maximum in no more than the same number of years as they would have done under existing arrangements.

* This transition assumes completion of probation. If current probationers have not completed the probationary period by 1 April 2002, they would remain on £17,870 and would then move to £19,000 immediately the probationary period had been completed.

---

[1] All new scales and ranges should be uprated to reflect the outcome of the current negotiation in the SJNC on a cost-of-living increase to apply from 1 April 2000 (see paragraph 5.33 above)

Existing Senior and Assistant Principal Teachers

Current salary	Salary on 01/08/00 after normal incremental progression	Transitional scale – 01/04/01	Salary on 01/08/01 after normal incremental progression on transitional scale	New salary – 01/04/02
£23,436	£24,117	£26,046	£26,775	£28,250
£24,117	£24,792	£26,775	N/A	£28,250
£24,792	N/A	£26,775	N/A	£28,250

Notes Senior Teachers and Assistant Principal Teachers will all move onto a transitional scale, involving an 8 per cent increase, on 1 April 2001, and will (where applicable) receive increments on 1 August 2000 and 1 August 2001. They will then be placed on the penultimate point of the new Chartered Teacher scale on 1 April 2002, involving a further uplift of 5.5 per cent for all.

However, some Assistant Principal Teachers will be assimilated to the new Principal Teacher scale (see below), depending on the functions of the posts they fill.

Existing Principal Teachers

School roll	Current salary	Transitional range – 01/04/01	School roll	New range – 01/04/02
Up to 300	£25,659	£27,712	**Up to 550**	£30,000
301 – 600	£26,508	£28,629		
601 – 800	£27,372	£29,562	**551 – 1050**	£32,500
801 – 1000	£28,215	£30,472		
1001 – 1300	£29,082	£31,409	**Over 1050**	£35,000
Over 1300	£29,934	£32,329		
Special Educational Needs	£25,998	£28,078		£30,000

Notes Principal Teachers will all move onto a transitional range, involving an 8 per cent increase, on 1 April 2001. Their place on the new range on 1 April 2002, which will in all cases involve a further increase, will be determined by the new size bands for school roll for the primary and secondary sectors.

Principal Teachers in Special Educational Needs schools will all move onto the £30,000 point on 1 April 2002.

Existing Assistant Headteachers

Sector	Current salary	Transitional range – 01/04/01	School roll	New range – 01/04/02
Primary	£28,176	£30,430	**Up to 150**	£30,000
			151 – 550	£34,000
Secondary	£32,886	£35,517	**551 – 1050**	£39,000
			Over 1050	£44,000
Special Educational Needs	£28,848	£31,156	**Up to 60**	£34,000
			61 – 100	£36,500
			Over 100	£39,000

Notes Assistant Headteachers will all move onto a transitional range, involving an 8 per cent increase, on 1 April 2001.

Their place on the new Depute Headteacher range to be introduced on 1 April 2002 will be determined by the new size bands for school roll shown above, with primary and secondary on the same range. For those current Assistant Headteachers (notably those in larger primary schools) whose placement on the new range would involve a further increase on 1 April 2002 of more than 6.5 per cent over their salary at 1 April 2001, the increase needed to reach the new range point will be staged over a further period.

Any current Assistant Headteacher whose salary on the new range would be less than he or she will receive from the move onto the transitional range on 1 April 2001 will have that salary (including the 8 per cent increase) conserved until the relevant salary overtakes it.

Existing Depute Headteachers

Sector	School roll	Current salary	Transitional range – 01/04/01	School roll	New range – 01/04/02
Primary	Up to 450	£28,848	£31,156	Up to 150	£30,000
	451 – 600	£29,523	£31,885	151 – 550	£34,000
	Over 600	£31,539	£34,062	551 – 1050	£39,000
				Over 1050	£44,000
Secondary	Up to 100	£32,886	£35,517		
	101 – 300	£33,567	£36,252		
	301 – 550	£34,377	£37,127		
	551 – 800	£35,505	£38,345		
	801 – 1050	£36,618	£39,547		
	1051 – 1300	£37,743	£40,762		
	1301 – 1550	£38,862	£41,971		
	Over 1050	£39,987	£43,186		
Special Educational Needs	Up to 60	£29,523	£31,885	Up to 60	£34,000
	61 – 100	£30,870	£33,340	61 – 100	£36,500
	101 – 140	£31,539	£34,062	Over 100	£39,000
	Over 140	£32,211	£34,788		

Notes Depute Headteachers will all move onto a transitional range, involving an 8 per cent increase, on 1 April 2001.

Their place on the new Depute Headteacher range to be introduced on 1 April 2002 will be determined by the new size bands for school roll shown above, with primary and secondary on the same range. For those (notably those in larger primary schools) whose placement on the new range would involve a further increase on 1 April 2002 of more than 6.5 per cent over their salary at 1 April 2001, the increase needed to reach the new range point will be staged over a further period.

Any current Depute Headteacher whose salary on the new range would be less than he or she will receive from the move onto the transitional range on 1 April 2001 will have that salary (including the 8 per cent increase) conserved until the relevant salary overtakes it.

Existing Headteachers

Sector	School roll	Current salary	Transitional range – 01/04/01	School roll	New range – 01/04/02
Primary	Up to 50	£28,848	£31,156	Up to 50	£36,000
	51 – 150	£30,870	£33,340	51 – 150	£40,000
	151 – 300	£32,211	£34,788	151 – 300	£44,000
	301 – 450	£33,567	£36,252	301 – 550	£47,500
	451 – 600	£36,618	£39,547	551 – 800	£51,000
	Over 600	£38,862	£41,971	801 – 1050	£54,000
				1051- 1300	£56,500
Secondary	Up to 100	£33,567	£36,252	1301- 1550	£59,000
	101 – 300	£37,743	£40,762	Over 1550	£61,500
	301 – 550	£41,109	£44,398		
	551 – 800	£43,350	£46,818		
	801 – 1050	£46,716	£50,453		
	1051- 1300	£48,960	£52,877		
	1301- 1550	£51,198	£55,294		
	Over 1550	£53,439	£57,714		
Combined		£31,539	£34,062		
		£33,567	£36,252		
		£37,743	£40,762		
		£41,109	£44,398		
		£43,350	£46,818		
Special Educational Needs	Up to 30	£30,870	£33,340	Up to 30	£40,000
	31 – 60	£32,886	£35,517	31 – 60	£44,000
	61 – 100	£34,377	£37,127	61 – 100	£45,750
	101 – 140	£36,618	£39,547	101 – 140	£47,500
	Over 140	£38,862	£41,971	Over 140	£51,000

Notes Headteachers will all move onto a transitional range, involving an 8 per cent increase, on 1 April 2001.

Their place on the new Headteacher range to be introduced on 1 April 2002 will be determined by the new size bands for school roll shown above, with primary and secondary on the same range. For those (notably those in larger primary schools) whose placement on the new range would involve a further increase on 1 April 2002 of more than 6.5 per cent over their salary at 1 April 2001, the increase needed to reach the new range point will be staged over a further period.

Any current Headteacher whose salary on the new range would be less than he or she will receive from the move onto the transitional range on 1 April 2001 will have that salary (including the 8 per cent increase) conserved until the relevant salary overtakes it.

With the integration of the ranges for the primary and secondary sectors, the formula used to determine the salaries of Headteachers of combined primary/secondary schools is no longer appropriate. Their salaries will be determined according to the new school roll bands when primary and secondary rolls are counted together.

Section 6:
Conditions of service

6.1   Teaching is a profession, and a profession of particular importance to society. Teachers' conditions of service should reflect that fact. In common with other professions, teachers have a commitment to their career; it is something they take pride in doing well. They have chosen it because they want to do it and believe they have an aptitude for it. Like other professionals, they must be expected to carry out their work with a sense of duty that ensures they do so to the best of their ability; and they must be accountable not only to their employers, but to those responsible for the children they teach.

6.2   This sense of duty and commitment will, however, be adversely affected if teachers feel that they are being asked to take on unreasonable burdens without adequate consideration of the stress and scale of the workload they imply. As a protection against such burdens, teachers' representatives have sought to limit workload by setting down limits in the national scheme of conditions of service on the maximum amount of time to be spent on particular activities. The practical consequence of this approach has been to introduce a high degree of complexity and rigidity into the system, and to make proper management of the teaching resource much harder.

The Yellow Book

6.3   Those members of the Committee who approached their task from a background in other professions were astonished at the level of prescriptive detail in the Scheme of Salaries and Conditions of Service for Teaching Staff in School Education, known as the Yellow Book. This scheme is legally binding throughout Scotland. There are a number of reasons why this degree of prescription has grown up, some of them historical: much of the detail followed the report of the Main Inquiry in 1986, which took place at a time of a serious dispute and "work to rule" by teachers. There have also been concerns about workload going back long beyond the Main Inquiry, however; and it may be that, because teachers' local authority employers were relatively remote, teachers and their representatives felt that these concerns were not fully recognised, and thus needed to be enshrined in law. It has also been suggested that teachers may not always have had confidence that their Headteachers would allocate work appropriately in the absence of such a framework: although the Committee did not encounter any instances of this in the course of its school visits.

6.4   The fact is, however, that this prescriptive approach has totally failed to limit workload pressures. This was very clear from the response to the Committee's consultation document: the vast majority of teachers considered workload to be among the most pressing problems facing the profession, and argued that workload had increased significantly in recent years. Both the EIS and the SSTA placed particular emphasis on this aspect of the current situation.

6.5   Teachers, like other professionals, often work well beyond their contractual working time because they are committed to their work. It was common ground on the part of all those who gave oral evidence to us, including the teachers' unions, that the conditions laid down in the Yellow Book were too prescriptive. The Committee thinks that they not only impose rigidities that are most undesirable, but that they have not served the interests of teachers well. Furthermore, we believe to lay down in minute detail how teachers are to spend their time is demeaning to their professional status; and may actually have served to undermine their image in the eyes of the public.

6.6   The Yellow Book sets out a wide range of conditions of service that apply to the employment of teachers and other professionals in the education service. The Committee has not attempted to comment on all of these. Many of them seem to us to be relevant and appropriate: but we have serious doubts as to whether they all need to be laid down in detail in a central statutory scheme. The Committee notes that the removal of the statutory basis of the SJNC has implications for the Yellow Book, in that any successor scheme will also be without statutory force. *The Committee recommends that in future core issues such as pay, main duties, overall working time, sickness and maternity leave, and discipline should continue to be determined nationally. However, it is for consideration whether other conditions of service should be agreed at national or local level. The Committee notes that Task Group 4 of the Millennium Review proposed an extension of the scope for local negotiation; and recommends that such flexibility should apply in any future framework.* We discuss the future negotiating mechanism in Section 8 of this report.

6.7   We have no recommendations to make in relation to the terms of service of educational psychologists and advisers, considering that they are not covered by our terms of reference.

6.8   In the paragraphs that follow we therefore focus principally on teachers' duties, workload and working time, class sizes, temporary contracts and cover for absence. Issues concerning quality assurance are dealt with in Section 7 of this report.

Teachers' duties

6.9   Any national scheme of conditions of service obviously needs to describe what a teacher's main duties should be. This description should encompass all of the activities which a teacher should normally be expected to undertake. But it should be stated in broad terms, taking account of the fact that teaching is a profession and giving a degree of scope for the exercise of professional discretion. Attempting to define teachers' duties in detail, while understandable in the context of the 1980s "work to rule", is bound to fail over the medium-term, and may well serve to make teachers much more conscious of rules, in many cases artificial, rather than relying on a sense of responsibility, judgement and common sense.

6.10   Many respondents to the Committee's consultation document argued that the current statement of teachers' duties set out in the Yellow Book no longer met the requirements of the service, because it did not cater adequately for flexible working, nor anticipate change to the education service. There has been a great deal of change in education, as in every other sphere, over the last decade; there will no doubt be more change in the future. Where such change arises from policy initiatives, it needs to be managed very carefully. (We make recommendations on this point below.) But any changes in the outside environment are likely to have an impact on teachers' activities; and any description of teachers' duties needs to allow for that.

6.11   At the same time, however, the Committee sees a genuine need for a statement of duties that protects teachers, by setting out those matters that should rightly be regarded as their responsibility, and those that should properly be done by others. Teachers throughout Scotland have told the Committee of their concern at the scale and breadth of their workload; and it is clearly right that they should concentrate their effort on work for which they are professionally trained. (We make recommendations on support staff to carry out other duties in Section 3 of this report.)

6.12 *The Committee therefore considers that the duties of all teachers should include: teaching assigned classes, together with the associated preparation and correction; developing the school curriculum; assessing, recording and reporting on the work of pupils; preparing pupils for examinations, and sharing responsibility for administering them; offering advice and guidance to pupils; promoting and safeguarding the health, welfare and safety of pupils; working in partnership with parents and other professional colleagues; undertaking appropriate continuing professional development in order to maintain and improve their skills and competences; participating with colleagues in planning, raising attainment, school self-improvement, and individual review (on which we make specific recommendations in Section 7 of this report); and contributing, together with colleagues, towards the good order and wider life of the school.*

6.13 *Teachers who are promoted to Principal Teacher and above should in addition have explicit responsibility for the leadership, good management and strategic direction of their department, faculty or for the school (depending on their level); curriculum development and quality assurance; the development of school policy for the behaviour management of pupils; the management and guidance of junior professional colleagues, in particular those still on probation; the review of junior colleagues' performance; the provision of advice to junior colleagues, as appropriate, on their career development and CPD needs; and, as appropriate, links with the wider community.*

6.14 *Responsibilities must, however, be balanced by rights. The Committee considers that all teachers should have the right to expect an enabling framework of resources, organisation, time management, strategic planning, consultation, personnel and professional support, high quality CPD and support from parents to assist them in carrying out their responsibilities.*

6.15 *The Committee recommends that broad descriptions along these lines should replace the existing detailed provisions of the national scheme; and that any more detailed job descriptions should be decided at local level, on the basis of specific needs relating to individual posts.*

Workload and working time

6.16 The Committee recognises that teaching is a demanding and at times stressful activity. The effort and concentration required when a teacher is in front of a class is intense: more intense, and more sustained, than that required in many other occupations. Of course, all jobs have their particular characteristics and stresses; and this tends to make comparison, particularly in relation to overall hours worked, invidious.

6.17 Nevertheless, the Committee was struck by the strength of feeling on this issue expressed in responses to the consultation document. And during the programme of visits to schools, the Committee was impressed by the evidence of commitment and long hours worked by very many teachers. Teachers from Shetland and the Outer Isles to the Central Belt and the Borders spoke of the increased burdens of the workload. Everywhere the points made were the same: much of this had to do with the number of initiatives coming from the Scottish Executive and the increased paperwork associated with them; and with developments in relation to pupil assessment. We heard no complaints that any of the initiatives were misguided: but it was said that some required a lot of work before they could be put into practice in schools. Particular criticism was directed at the materials produced to support the introduction of Higher Still; and the lack of materials for teachers employed in Gaelic medium education was also said to be a problem. The general complaint, however, was that there were just so many new initiatives, documents and requirements for information from the Executive (including Her Majesty's Inspectorate) that staff were becoming overwhelmed.

6.18 *The Committee therefore recommends strongly that the Scottish Executive, when considering any new initiative of whatever kind, should ensure that the profession is properly consulted on its design; and should evaluate its likely impact on workload. Where this evaluation reveals that a significant increase is likely, the Executive should consider the allocation of additional resources to implement the initiative, or should defer its introduction. Once initiatives have been introduced, their implementation should be kept under regular review so that unintended consequences in terms of workload can be addressed. Moreover, there should be a mechanism within the Executive for co-ordinating the various activities which will impact on schools, with a view to ensuring coherence, consistency and the greatest possible degree of streamlining.*

6.19 *The Committee also considers that the Executive should commission an independent "bureaucracy audit", to be carried out by independent consultants, to look at:*

- *the amount, form and frequency of information required from schools by the Scottish Executive Education Department, Her Majesty's Inspectorate and local authorities;*

- *the benefit it generates for pupils, parents and policy-makers;*

- *and to make recommendations on the design of processes with a view to reducing the burden on teachers arising from information demands.*

6.20 *The Committee notes that the Executive has recently launched a public consultation exercise on national education priorities. In our view, this provides a much-needed opportunity to take stock of the current situation; to review the interaction of the various disparate policy initiatives launched in recent years, including the associated administrative and financing arrangements; and to develop a coherent and transparent development plan at national level, which will provide a clear and stable framework for the education service. The Committee urges the Executive to make full use of this opportunity.*

Working hours

6.21 The arrangements for working hours are at present highly prescriptive. In large measure this follows the report of the Main Inquiry, but for the reasons already given we do not think this appropriate for a profession which, like other professions, should be trusted to manage itself flexibly.

6.22 The present agreement specifies:

- A working week for 'planning purposes' of 35 hours

- 27.5 hours per week to be spent in school

- Maximum class contact time of 25 hours in primary schools, 23.5 hours in secondary schools and 22.5 hours in special schools

- 30 hours a year for parent meetings, to include preparatory work and travelling time, with up to six such meetings within the pupil year

- 50 hours within the teacher's working year for planned activities related to wider educational needs, including curricular development, in-service training, inter-school liaison, professional development and meetings with colleagues.

6.23   Apart from the lack of flexibility that this specification implies, and its incompatibility with a truly professional approach to work - upon which we have already commented - the Committee thinks that it serves teachers, headteachers and the public very badly. For teachers, it has not afforded meaningful protection from increasing workload or longer hours, because their sense of duty and commitment overrides what is laid down in the agreement. For headteachers, it has meant that planning necessary collegiate activities without disrupting the pupils' day has been extremely difficult. And for the public, who tend to focus on time actually spent in school, it contributes to the (misguided) impression that teachers have short hours as well as long holidays, an impression that has been damaging to the esteem in which the profession is held.

6.24   As far as class contact time is concerned, a survey carried out by the EIS among some of its members, and included in its evidence to the Committee, showed that, on average, teachers taught significantly less than the maximum class contact time: 16 hours in secondary schools and 20 hours in primary. We think this is not surprising, considering that it is an average, whereas the agreement stipulates a maximum, and that the more senior teachers, from Principal Teacher upwards, spend time in management-related functions that maingrade teachers spend in the classroom. But if one takes class contact time at its maximum, 23.5 hours, in secondary schools, then adds to it a reasonable amount of time for preparation and correction and the various other duties required of teachers, it is in practice difficult if not impossible to fit everything within the existing working week. In the primary sector, where the maximum class contact time is 25 hours, this may be even more difficult.

6.25   It is not surprising, therefore, that teachers are found to work well in excess of the hours for which they are "contracted" to work. The survey carried out by the EIS suggested that, on average, teachers reported working about 42 hours a week. This finding is confirmed by a study carried out for the Committee by Professors Bell and Elias of the Universities of Stirling and Warwick, using the Labour Force Survey. Their report is reproduced as Appendix B of this report (see below).

6.26   We have considered a number of approaches to this problem. One possibility would be to recognise that teachers are doing more than the 35 hours assumed in the current agreement, and to lengthen the contract week accordingly. Such an approach was proposed by the Main Committee, but in the context of lengthening the week to bring it into line with other local authority employees. Any further lengthening would put teachers out of line with comparable groups both in local authorities and central government: but it might possibly be justified, on the grounds that, although teachers work very hard in the school term, they have longer holidays than other professionals. However, such an approach would also involve an adjustment to pay and would inevitably be costly to implement.

6.27   An alternative approach would be to recommend a significant and sustained increase in the number of teaching staff, so as to reduce the class contact hours and increase the time available to teachers for their other tasks. Given the lead times involved in training new entrants to the profession, and the existing need to recruit a growing number of teachers to replace those reaching the end of their careers, such an increase would be difficult to achieve in the short- to medium-term. It might also be difficult to explain to the general public, who might perceive it as implying that teachers will spend less time teaching.   Finally, it would also be expensive. Bearing in mind that funds available to the Scottish Executive are limited, and that money spent on this would inevitably reduce the amount available to finance our other recommendations aimed at putting the profession on a better basis for the future – including recommendations on freeing up time for teaching and improving pay - the Committee was not convinced that such an approach was the right one.

6.28 The study by Professors Bell and Elias shows that teachers are not alone in working well beyond their notional 35 hour week. Indeed, as the chart below shows, their position is by no means out of the ordinary compared with other professions. The Committee believes that if the other recommendations in this report are implemented, particularly those for support staff, they will reduce the amount of work that teachers have to undertake in their own time: but it also accepts that, like other professional people, teachers will probably always work beyond the hours stated in their contracts. *We therefore recommend that 35 hours should continue to be the basis for the contractual week.*

Figure 1: Basic hours, unpaid and paid overtime

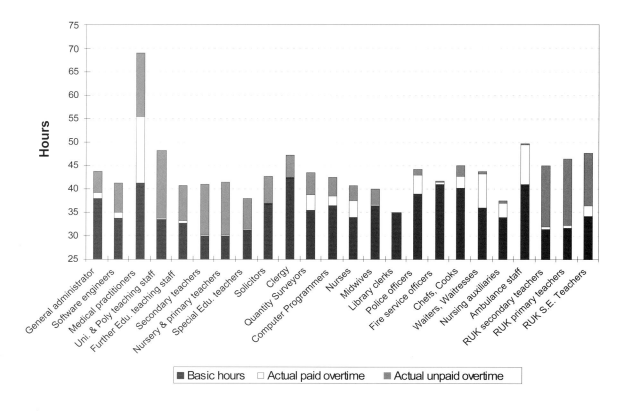

6.29 Some of those who gave evidence to the Committee, and notably CoSLA, argued that the only other component of working time that should be specified was class contact time; and that all of the difference between that and the total of 35 hours should be under the control of the headteacher to deploy in the best interests of the school.

6.30 We do not think that would be satisfactory. Preparation and correction is just as important as class contact, to which it is essentially related. The Main Committee recognised this, but did not specify an overall fixed time for it because it varied between subjects and between individual teachers, and depended on circumstances. Nevertheless we recognise that there is a concern among teachers that if all of the balance between class contact time and the contractual working week were at the disposal of headteachers, the amount of time available for preparation and correction might tend to be eroded by other tasks, increasing the amount of work which needs to be undertaken elsewhere.

6.31   *We therefore recommend a simple arrangement. Within the 35 hour contract week, 30 hours would be allocated to "core" activities comprising class contact and preparation and correction. The balance, five hours, should be available for the range of other collective activities contributing to the wider life of the school, to be decided by the staff in each school on a collegiate basis, led by the headteacher as overall manager and the person ultimately accountable for the activities of the school. The use of this collective time should in principle be decided annually. It might be necessary to deploy it flexibly over the course of the school year, for example to deal with peaks of activity at assessment time or at the start of the session. Equally, in some cases it might not be necessary to use the equivalent of the whole five hours. The key point is that collegiate activities should be planned, agreed, deployed and used collectively for the benefit of the whole school.*

6.32   The Committee does not propose that within the 30 hours of "core" time there should be a single binding figure specified for class contact time, because we do not think that there is a single straightforward mathematical relationship between the number of hours of class contact and the time required for preparation and correction: but neither would it wish to see the maximum amount of class contact increased. We consider it a better approach to look at class contact and the associated preparation and correction as a whole, because they are inextricably linked and they are also the key activities for which the teacher is individually responsible. This also has the incidental advantage of giving the public a fairer picture of a teacher's "core" workload than a constant emphasis on the smaller figure for class contact.

6.33   The Committee recognises that 30 hours may not provide a very large margin for preparation and correction for those teachers who may be working at the present maximum level of class contact time. But the time required for preparation and correction varies greatly depending on circumstances; and at the very least, the arrangement we propose would provide a reasonable minimum for this purpose. Moreover, it would be open to schools to decide to increase the amount of time available for this as part of their deployment of their overall time resource.

6.34   The Committee also recognises that many teachers prefer to do much of their preparation and correction at home. We have no difficulty of principle with this. There is no intrinsic reason why preparation and correction should be carried out on the school premises; and, as some teachers have pointed out to us, after an intensive day of teaching, they can do the job better if they get home, have a break, and settle down to preparation and correction in the evening in the relative peace and quiet of their own home. We believe that this flexibility is greatly valued by teachers, and we do not wish to change that: unless, of course, staff in individual schools decide that they wish to do otherwise. We recognise, however, that some collective activities have to take place outside the pupil day: time for these will have to be agreed at school level.

6.35   The five hours for school activities to be decided on by staff on a collegiate basis offers the prospect of a real change from existing arrangements. It may require quite a change of culture, both on the part of staff and some headteachers. The Committee was impressed in the course of its visits to schools by the collegiate way in which some schools operated. Not all of them do so, of course; and although we did not come across it in any of the schools we visited, we have the impression that in some instances there may be a lack of trust between the rest of the profession and headteachers. The Committee finds this most regrettable; and hopes that the introduction of the Scottish Qualification for Headship will help to dispel any doubts about the leadership skills of headteachers. In the Committee's view, teachers and headteachers must work together to take forward their shared educational task in the best interests of Scotland's children. We also think that, if teachers want to be taken seriously as professionals, they must be prepared to take responsibility collectively for all the school duties that are required of them.

6.36 Finally, we see no need to specify any difference in these arrangements between primary and secondary schools. At present primary schools have a longer maximum class contact time than secondary. Whatever the justification for this may have been at one time, we think it no longer applies. The EIS made this point in its submission to the Committee. *We therefore recommend that there should be 30 hours for core activities in primary schools, the same as for secondaries; and that maximum class contact time should also be the same. We recognise that this will take some time to achieve, and that it may require some additional teachers in the primary sector. In this context, we would also see advantage in providing a greater number of specialist staff to the primary schools, perhaps on a cluster basis, in recognition of the breadth of the curriculum that now has to be covered; and we recommend that this option be examined urgently.*

The working year

6.37 The working year for teachers is at present 195 days, of which 190 days coincide with the school year for pupils; the remaining five days beyond the pupil year are intended to accommodate development activities planned by the local authority, principally in-service training. These figures were determined following the report of the Main Committee, the previous school year having been 200 days.

6.38 The Committee has set out its views on the importance of continuing professional development (CPD) in Section 3 of this report. It is also aware that a teacher's frequent absence from class to attend courses is immensely disruptive to the work of the school, and to the progress made by pupils in particular. It also imposes heavy demands either on other teachers within the school or on supply teachers, of which there is increasingly a scarcity about which we comment in Section 3 of this report. We therefore think it necessary to limit as far as possible teacher absences from class, while at the same time giving added emphasis to CPD, if overall educational standards are to improve.

6.39 To reduce the pupil year further in the interests of CPD would, in our view, be unacceptable in terms of pupils' education. We think it would also be unacceptable to parents. We consider that, in the interests of their personal and professional development, teachers should be able to invest more of their own time in developing their skills and competences, provided that:

- there is a real improvement in the quality and relevance of CPD activities available;

- courses and materials are properly accredited at national level;

- adequate resources are made available to finance it;

- and that the career structure in the teaching profession delivers recognition and reward for teachers' own investment in the process.

6.40 *We therefore recommend that a further five days or their equivalent be allocated to continuing professional development. This time should be made available flexibly either from time beyond the pupil year or from time beyond the 35 hour week.*

Class size

6.41 Many of those who sent written submissions to the Committee and teachers we met on our school visits argued for a reduction in class sizes. We are aware that it is the policy of the Scottish Executive to reduce class sizes in the early years of primary school. We very much welcome that development. We also note that the Executive is currently consulting on the provisions relating to class size in the Schools (Scotland) Code. To reduce class sizes further would require additional teaching and building resources; it would also be very expensive. Any new initiative to reduce class sizes would therefore be likely, in the Committee's view, to be at the expense of our other recommendations, to which we attach greater importance.

6.42 We also note that class sizes in Scotland, as shown in the table below, are significantly smaller than in England or Wales. We believe that this may be largely accounted for by smaller class sizes in Scotland's more sparsely populated areas that bring down the average. But we nevertheless believe that this would also make it difficult to secure the finance to reduce class sizes in Scotland further.

Average class sizes in publicly-funded schools in 1998/99

	Primary One teacher classes	All classes	Secondary One teacher classes	All classes
Scotland	**24.9**	**24.9**		**19.2**
England	27.4	27.6	21.9	22.0
Wales		25.6		20.6

Notes Data for special schools not available.
Secondary data for Scotland relates to 1997/98.

Pupil/teacher ratios in publicly-funded schools in 1998/99

	Primary	Secondary	Special
Scotland	**19.4**	**13.0**	**4.4**
England	23.5	17.0	6.7
Wales	23.0	16.5	6.9

Notes Calculations based on full-time equivalents.

Number of teachers in publicly-funded schools per 100,000 population in 1998/99

	Primary	Secondary	Special
Scotland	**445**	**477**	**38**
England	389	376	28
Wales	443	422	19

Notes Calculations based on full-time equivalents.

Source: Scottish Executive

6.43   Moreover, the recommendations we have made for additional support in the classroom, and in schools more generally, should make a significant positive contribution to the quality of education in Scotland. They should go a long way towards easing the pressures on teachers arising from large classes. *We do not, therefore, propose any changes to the existing maximum class sizes as part of our report.*

6.44   *The Committee does, however, recognise the sensitivity of the issue of class sizes; and therefore recommends that the Scottish Executive commission independent research into the relationship between class sizes and individual educational attainment.*

Absence cover

6.45   The Committee received a number of representations on problems resulting from the existing national agreement on absence cover. This requires a supply teacher to be engaged if a teacher is away for no more than three days, regardless of whether the absence can be more effectively covered from within the school or whether the supply teacher available is suitable to fill the vacancy. In extreme cases we were told that the absence of a senior member of the management team may trigger the engagement of a supply teacher even when the senior teacher was undertaking very little classroom work. We understand that most local authorities now have local agreements to cover absence and we think this more appropriate. *We therefore recommend that the existing national agreement be deleted.*

Transfer of temporary teachers to the permanent staff

6.46   The Yellow Book currently provides that where a teacher has been employed for a year on a temporary contract, he or she is entitled to be employed on a permanent basis. The Committee received representations from the local authorities that this provision should be deleted from any future scheme, because it does not have regard to the availability of permanent contracts; and because it runs counter to the principle of free competition for all posts which employment legislation requires authorities to operate. The EIS argued in its evidence to the Committee that this provision was a useful protection for teachers, and should be retained. The Committee shares the EIS's concern about the widespread use of temporary contracts. We have reservations, however, about the effectiveness and appropriateness of this provision in achieving this aim, because in practice the use of temporary contracts is widespread. *The Committee therefore recommends that this provision be deleted in any new national scheme of conditions of service: but we have also recommended in Section 3 of this report that use of temporary contracts should be limited to the strict minimum.*

Timing

6.47   *The Committee considers that modernisation of conditions of service in the ways described above is the counterpart of its recommendations for a new salary structure. It therefore recommends that all of the changes proposed should come into effect at the same time as the new salary scales on 1 April 2002.*

Section 7:
Ensuring quality

7.1 Effective learning and teaching in schools ultimately depends upon the professional skills of teachers, and on the quality of support available to enable them to maintain and update their skills. In Section 3 of this report, the Committee has made a number of specific recommendations which relate to developing and supporting the quality of the profession. In particular, these are intended to enhance teachers' knowledge and skills; and to make it possible for them to concentrate their efforts on the key elements of teaching and learning, and on other tasks which only they can do. They include recommendations on:

- initial teacher training;

- improved arrangements for induction into the profession and probation;

- giving greater emphasis to continuing professional development, to allow teachers to refresh and improve their skills;

- options for older teachers to "wind down" by taking on a less demanding job, going part-time, or widening the pool of supply teachers, thus facilitating the move of younger teachers into key positions;

- and on increasing support staff, so that teachers are enabled to concentrate on their key functions.

7.2 All of this will go a long way to promoting a focus on quality. But in addition in Sections 4 and 5 we recommend a career and salary structure which will reward and recognise excellence in the classroom, including creation of the new status of Chartered and Advanced Chartered Teacher founded on teaching excellence, CPD and classroom-based research; while in Section 6, we have sought to give priority within the working week to activities relating directly to teaching and learning.

7.3 However, these measures would of themselves be inadequate without a framework to ensure that teachers' performance is the subject of regular and structured review. The main purpose of such a system is to give teachers an opportunity to discuss and review their work at regular intervals with more senior colleagues. This will help to ensure quality, by giving teachers the opportunity to talk about their aspirations and problems, strengths and weaknesses. For younger teachers, it will give them the benefit of advice from those with longer experience. It will enable training needs to be identified, appropriate development activity discussed, and priorities and objectives set for CPD. And it will ensure that individual performance and development remain at the centre of the education system.

7.4 We realise that a thorough system of performance review will be new to much of the teaching profession. Until relatively recently, the tradition has been for teachers to see their work in the classroom as primarily a matter for their own individual judgement. Professional discretion is an essential element of teaching: but it must be supplemented by review and discussion. It may take some time for attitudes to change. But other professions have for many years benefited from review systems; and we see considerable advantage in the introduction of such a system for the teaching profession. Moreover, we consider it necessary for the good management of the profession, and essential if the public as parents and taxpayers are to be confident that standards are being maintained and improved. This section of our report therefore considers issues of performance management.

Performance management

7.5   A performance management system for the teaching profession must serve two main functions: to enable individual teachers, irrespective of grade, to gain a clear picture of how they are performing, identifying in the process areas where they may need additional support or training; and to ensure that each teacher's work contributes in the most effective manner to the overall objectives of the school. One of the key roles of the management team in schools should be to monitor performance throughout the school and provide feedback to members of staff. This process should be a continuous one, based on regular informal contact; but it should also be supplemented by a regular and structured review.

7.6   The Committee understands that in January 1998 the Scottish Office issued guidelines for staff development and review systems to local authorities, with a request that all teachers should receive at least one review interview by June 1999. From information provided to us by the Scottish Executive, it appears that few local authorities met this deadline; and that several had yet to do so at the end of the year. Moreover, in the course of its programme of school visits, the Committee was struck by how few teachers reported having participated in a review. It was also noticeable that in the consultation process, very few respondents and none of the main organisations involved in the Scottish education service referred to the issue of performance review.

7.7   *The Committee finds this state of affairs most unsatisfactory, and therefore recommends that the Scottish Executive, in close co-operation with the local authorities and consulting the teaching unions, take immediate steps to introduce universal review procedures in line with best practice identified across Scotland.* We are conscious that the environment of a school has its special characteristics: in small schools, in particular, colleagues will know one another very well, including their strengths and weaknesses. It is important that a review system should take account of the particular circumstances of the Scottish education service. It would be a mistake simply to transfer across an appraisal system that works for another profession. But the Committee is aware that systems have been introduced with apparent success in some parts of Scotland: these should serve as exemplars for other areas.

7.8   A review system should involve the following elements:

- it should be based on an agreed job description and individual personal objectives, relating both to the overall objectives of the department and school and to the professional development of the individual;

- it should result in a formal document signed and commented upon by both reviewee and reviewer, who would normally be the reviewee's immediate line manager, for example a PT for a maingrade teacher, a Depute Headteacher for a PT and the Headteacher for a member of senior management team including both Depute Headteachers and the Senior Administrative Officer.   The reports should be countersigned as far as possible by a Depute Headteacher or by the Headteacher;

- No teacher should carry out a review of a colleague before he or she has also been the subject of a review;

- Headteachers should also be subject to a review, probably carried out by the Director of Education of the relevant authority or his or her nominee;

- there should in all cases be a provision for appeal or outside review;

- the process must be transparent, understandable and not excessively time-consuming;

- to make the system effective, appropriate training for all staff involved should be carried out as soon as possible.

7.9   In order to be meaningful, the review process must be accompanied by appropriate provision and opportunity for CPD; and must be relevant to the career of the individual teacher.   A satisfactory review record should be considered necessary for promotion. The Committee has also made explicit provision for this in its proposals for a programme for the achievement of Chartered and Advanced Chartered Teacher status.

Dealing with under-performance

7.10   The main function of a system of review is to help staff to improve their performance and identify training needs: but it also has a crucial role to play in dealing with cases where a teacher's performance, for whatever reason, is falling below acceptable standards. It should facilitate the spotting of potential problems at an early stage; and should provide an appropriate framework for one-to-one discussion and identification of any remedial action that may be needed. In this way it should prevent serious problems from developing.

7.11   However, any system must be supplemented by appropriate, effective and transparent procedures for dealing with the small number of cases where performance remains persistently below required levels. The provision of suitable support for the individual concerned should be the first priority: but in some instances it may be necessary to move a teacher to different or less onerous duties; and from time to time it may be appropriate to proceed to disciplinary action.   Procedures for dealing with cases of under-performance need to be based on clear and agreed standards for capability. *The Committee has taken careful note in this regard of the HMI report "Meeting Professional Standards"; and it strongly urges the Executive to press ahead, in close co-operation with other interested parties, with the definition of such national standards and the issuance of guidance on their use.*

Misconduct

7.12   If ensuring that there are effective means of dealing with under-performance is an important element of ensuring quality within the teaching profession, then effective procedures for dealing with misconduct are also essential, both for the good management of the education service and for the reassurance of parents. Given the key role played by teachers in the development of Scotland's children, improper behaviour clearly cannot be tolerated in our schools. The Committee attaches the highest importance to effective and fair procedures for dealing with misconduct.

Disciplinary procedures

7.13   The Committee notes that in the HMI report "Meeting Professional Standards" the headteachers surveyed were reported as pointing to difficulties in taking effective action: the Committee heard similar messages from some headteachers in the course of its consultation. It was put to us that disciplinary procedures were excessively slow and cumbersome.

7.14 Our attention was also drawn to the fact that in extreme cases where dismissal is proposed, the decision currently rests not with a senior representative of the local authority employer, such as the Director of Education, but with the elected members of the authority's Education Committee. Whilst understanding that elected members are accountable to local voters for the education service in their region, the Committee does not think that these arrangements, which differ from those applying to other areas of local government, are appropriate. It has been suggested that the current situation may in part be the unintended result of the timing of local authority restructuring and of a sequence of amendments to the relevant legislation.

7.15 The Committee notes that the employers' side of the SJNC has drawn up a new model disciplinary procedure resembling that in place for other local authority employees. It also notes that discussion is under way under the leadership of the Advisory Conciliation and Arbitration Service with a view to drawing up more streamlined disciplinary procedures for teachers; and that the Executive is working with other interested parties on standards for capability and conduct and advice for their implementation. *The Committee very much welcomes these developments, and urges the relevant parties to agree on a new framework as quickly as possible. The Committee considers that, in those few extreme cases where dismissal is deemed necessary, the decision should rest with the relevant Director of Education, subject to an appeals procedure. Since professional issues may be involved, and since a teacher's registration with the GTC might be at stake, we consider that appeals should be heard by a panel including members with appropriate expertise and experience in the field of education.*

Section 8:
Future negotiating mechanism

8.1 At the time he announced the creation of this Committee of Inquiry, the Minister for Children and Education announced his intention to remove the statutory basis of the Scottish Joint Negotiating Committee for Teaching Staff in School Education (SJNC), which since 1982 has been the body charged with setting pay and conditions of service for Scotland's teachers. This decision was apparently based on his view that the SJNC had failed either to deliver the modernisation of conditions of service sought by employers or to secure the salary increases wanted by teachers; and that it was not necessary for teachers' terms and conditions of employment to be laid down in statute. In particular, it was noted that Scottish teachers' salaries had not kept pace with those of teachers in England and Wales since the Main Inquiry (see Section 5); and that there had been no significant change in conditions of service since that time.

8.2 The Minister therefore called on the Committee to consider *"the future arrangements for determining teachers' pay and conditions in Scotland"*; and he has now made formal proposals to remove the statutory basis of the SJNC in the Standards in Scotland's Schools Etc. Bill currently before the Scottish Parliament.

8.3 ***The Committee therefore considers that the retention of the SJNC in its current form is not before it for consideration.*** It should, however, be noted that a significant number of respondents to the Committee's consultation exercise, particularly teachers, disagreed with the Minister's decision and called for the SJNC to be retained.

8.4 There are four broad approaches which it has been suggested could be taken to determining teachers' pay and conditions: a system of local bargaining between individual authorities and local teaching unions; a system of index-linking; the establishment of a national pay review body; or a system of national collective bargaining. Each has potential advantages and disadvantages.

8.5 Local bargaining would allow authorities the flexibility to deal with specific local conditions, and could encourage innovation in dealing with particular teacher shortages or rewarding excellence. Pay and working arrangements which might be appropriate in central Edinburgh, for example, may not be appropriate in Shetland or Orkney. Where there was a need to negotiate nationally on particular issues, this could still be done.

8.6 However, allowing the development of differing pay and conditions in different regions could lead to direct and ultimately damaging competition between individual authorities for teachers, creating or exaggerating disparities in education provision between regions; and it could have a detrimental effect on the profession as a whole. Moreover, there is reason to believe that local arrangements for what is essentially a national education service might be open to legal challenge under employment law.

8.7 The vast majority of individual respondents to the Committee's consultation who addressed this issue rejected local bargaining, most of them on the grounds that a local approach would lead inexorably to inequalities in provision. CoSLA and the teaching unions also rejected a decentralised approach. And the Minister has made clear to the Scottish Parliament that he supports the principle of a national framework for pay and conditions. The Committee shares this view. *It therefore rejects the idea that pay and core conditions of service should be the subject of local bargaining.*

8.8 This is not to say, however, that there is no scope for local variation on national conditions: a point picked up by a number of respondents to the consultation. As noted earlier, the current scheme of conditions of service allows some scope for local agreements with local authorities, and local arrangements have in practice been negotiated on absence cover in many areas.

8.9 Depending on the formula used, index-linking could be a transparent and effective way of protecting the value of teachers' salaries over time and, if linked to an appropriate indicator of pay movements, would protect teachers' salaries from erosion: but index-linking is inflexible, takes no account of developments in the wider economy and would not allow for any evolution of conditions of service in the light of changing circumstances. *Because of this inflexibility, the Committee does not recommend a system of index-linking.*

8.10 A pay review body has a number of possible attractions. Such a body generally consists of a group of individuals independent of government or political parties, selected – sometimes from a wide range of backgrounds - for their personal achievements or specific expertise; and, more importantly, their ability to analyse issues, take and weigh evidence and reach considered conclusions and recommendations. The major argument in favour of a pay review body is that it could take a detached and unbiased view of all the issues, and could reach conclusions based on evidence from the full range of interested parties. A pay review body might take the debate out of the political arena, and might reduce the risk of threats of industrial action or disputes. It might be better placed than the SJNC has been to obtain the data essential for informed decisions over pay. It might also be better able to protect teachers' salaries from the erosion they have suffered in recent years than a process of negotiation; and, depending on its remit, a review body might also facilitate change and innovation, because it would not be subject to a veto by one or other of the interested parties.

8.11 A large number of individual respondents to the consultation favoured the establishment of an independent body, for all of these reasons. It should be added that this approach was recommended by the last Committee of Inquiry under Sir Peter Main; and that since Main reported a pay review body has been set up for teachers in England and Wales.

8.12 On the other hand, a pay review body would effectively take decisions on pay out of the hands of the local authority employers, who are formally responsible to the local electorate for school performance – although it seems to the Committee that the public look increasingly to central government, rather than to the local authorities, for action in this respect. It would also reduce the ability of teachers, through their union representatives, to influence the process of how their pay is determined.

8.13 The question of responsibility for implementation of a pay review body's recommendations also arises. Local authorities are teachers' employers: but the Scottish Executive finances about 80 per cent of their expenditure through the Scottish Block. If the review body were to report to local authorities, its recommendations would presumably have to be subject to a negotiation between authorities and the Executive over funding before those recommendations could be implemented. If, on the other hand, the review body reported to the Executive, and Scottish Ministers had responsibility for deciding on its recommendations, there would be widespread concern in local authorities about the imposition of salary increases without corresponding guarantees of additional finance. This would again engender a debate between local authorities and the Scottish Executive about funding. Some Committee members saw merit in explicit debate about funding teachers' pay. But the majority of the Committee saw this as a potential source of considerable and damaging uncertainty and friction.

8.14 *On the basis of the current shared responsibility for financing the Scottish education system, the majority of the Committee does not recommend the establishment of a review body to determine the pay and conditions of Scottish teachers. But a minority view on the Committee, and one strongly held, is that a pay review body would be the better option for the future; and that this would be the best mechanism to provide the stability which the teaching profession needs so critically.*

8.15 Collective bargaining (of which the SJNC is, of course, one variant) is a model which is used for other local government employees and widely in both the public and private sectors. The main advantages are that the parties involved feel more in control of, and involved in, the process. The ability to represent the views of their members directly to the other party involved in the negotiation is felt to be very important, not least from the standpoint of maintaining credibility in their members' eyes.

8.16 Its disadvantages are that the process is highly politicised; is dependent on the goodwill of the participants, and can often end in stalemate; and that, because agreements tend to reflect the lowest common denominator acceptable to all of the parties, collective bargaining does not facilitate reform. Moreover, in the case of teachers, the ability of the employers' side to respond meaningfully to financial demands is extremely limited without the support of the Executive, making negotiations on significant changes to terms and conditions needed for the future unlikely to succeed. Nevertheless, this is a mechanism with which the parties are familiar and are keen to see continued.

8.17 In the view of the Committee, it is essential that future arrangements fulfil four basic conditions:

- They must be transparent, and involve all the main stakeholders;
- They must facilitate change and reform where it is needed, but also provide stability and certainty;
- They must prevent teachers' salaries falling, so that the profession is no longer able to recruit, retain and motivate high-quality staff;
- And, above all, they must allow the profession to escape the cycle of salary stagnation, periodic crises and the establishment of Committees of Inquiry like this one to seek to resolve them.

8.18 *With this in mind, the majority of the Committee makes the following recommendations:*

- *That teachers' pay should be determined by collective bargaining, in the form of a national bargaining committee;*
- *That this committee should generally work on an annual cycle, but with the discretion to negotiate two- or three-year settlements should it so choose;*
- *That there should, however, be flexibility for local negotiation between individual authorities and local unions, on the whole range of issues identified in the report of Task Group 4 of the Millennium Review, subject to notifying the national bargaining committee for approval on core issues;*

- *That the bargaining committee should be composed of representatives of the local authority employers; of the teaching unions, including the Headteachers' associations not currently represented in the SJNC; and of the Scottish Executive, as full participants in the negotiation;*

- *That the agreements reached in this body need not be enacted in statute. Employment law should provide sufficient safeguards against abuse;*

- *And finally, that in addition to the bargaining committee, the Minister for Children and Education should establish a small independent body which should carry out a three-yearly review of salaries, whose reports and recommendations should be delivered to all parties in the bargaining committee and made public. This review should compare the evolution of teachers' salaries against a range of comparator occupations over the preceding period, and should incorporate a pay levels check against a range of other occupations, based on a job evaluation exercise; it should also examine developments in relation to the supply of teachers. The body should have discretion to look at how conditions of service are operating, and whether adjustments are required; and should be able to submit reports and detailed recommendations to the bargaining committee for consideration.*

Section 9:
Costs, savings and next steps

9.1 We have sought to cost our proposals for a new salary structure on the basis of payroll information given to us by CoSLA, which is based on their most recent available salary survey. We estimate that the overall additional cost in salary terms, on the basis of the staff numbers in that survey, would be £96 million[1] in the financial year 2001/2002; an additional £84 million in 2002/2003; £11 million in 2003/2004; and £12 million in 2004/2005. Once fully implemented, the annual cost of our recommendations on salaries will be of the order of £190 million.

9.2 The costs of our proposals for Chartered Teacher status clearly depend on the level of take-up. For each 1,000 experienced teachers passing successfully through the scheme, the additional salary cost would be £750,000 a year. We have not sought to estimate the cost of Chartered Teachers embarking on the route to Advanced Chartered status because it will depend on the number achieving Chartered status, the timing, and the decisions of individuals on whether to enter this demanding scheme.

9.3 Our proposal for the creation of Senior Administrative Officer posts in schools would cost about £33 million a year, assuming one for each school over 500 pupils and one for every five smaller schools.

9.4 As far as classroom assistants are concerned, we estimate that the Scottish Executive's commitment to a target of 5,000 will cost an additional £39 million a year in salaries, on the basis of the current average. Meeting the more ambitious objective we propose for the primary sector, which will require about another 1,000 classroom assistants, would cost another £11 million. We are not in a position to estimate the costs of introducing a new cadre of para-professionals in the secondary sector.

9.5 We have made no estimates for the cost of provision of additional CPD.

9.6 Taken together, these costs are significant; and are clearly far in excess of what local authorities can be expected to raise from within their existing and planned allocations. However, we consider that our proposals should also generate a variety of savings, which are difficult to quantify but which should be considerable:

- Over time, we would expect to see some reduction in the number of promoted posts as a result of the move to a new four-band career structure and the more collegiate approach we are proposing;

- the creation of Senior Administrative Officers, additional classroom assistants and para-professionals should free up valuable management and teaching time at all levels of the profession;

- our proposals to increase the amount of time allocated to CPD outside the school day and year should significantly reduce the cost of providing supply cover for

---

[1] All figures exclude employers' costs, but include the costs of normal annual increments during the transition period

planned absences. The savings here could be considerable: we understand that the current cost of supply cover is well in excess of £100 million.

9.7 More importantly, by promoting flexibility, collegiality and CPD and recognising and rewarding excellence in the classroom, we believe that our proposals should make a real difference to the quality of teaching and learning in our schools. This in turn should improve the productivity, flexibility and competitiveness of the Scottish economy, increase Scotland's prosperity, and deliver wide-ranging benefits for Scottish society as a whole. We therefore believe that they amply justify the additional expenditure now to put the profession on a sound basis for the 21st century. If we are to reap the benefits of a first-class education service, we must make the necessary investment now.

9.8 The Committee feels very strongly that the recommendations in this report must be taken as a whole. Our proposed new salary structure, which will involve significant increases in pay for most Scottish teachers, must be seen as the counterpart of our proposals for modernisation of conditions of service, and for a more flexible, collegiate approach towards education in Scotland's schools. Our recommendations for improving the support given to teachers, and for better CPD, with more time to undertake it, will play an important part in reducing stress, managing workload and raising attainment. And we consider an effective system of performance review to be an essential element of raising standards and ensuring quality in the education service. Our recommendations have been conceived as a package; none of them can properly be considered in isolation from the others. We would therefore be strongly opposed to any attempt to take a selective approach to our report.

9.9 However, we recognise that, as well as a substantial amount of additional finance, implementing the recommendations we make in this report will require considerable time and effort on the part of a number of bodies. It will also need a lot of discussion and consultation before new arrangements can be put in place. We therefore call on the Scottish Executive to consult the main parties on this report as quickly as possible; to agree a framework for taking our recommendations forward; and to publish a timetable for action.

Summary of recommendations[1]

Section 3: Developing and supporting the teaching profession

PROFESSIONAL DEVELOPMENT

Initial training

3.5 The Executive should commission a review of the design of initial training courses, and specifically:

- More attention should be given in courses to issues of pupil management, to putting the theories of teaching and learning into practice and to other new needs such as the impact of new technologies and the teaching of modern languages in primary schools;

- Teacher education institution (TEI) staff should be required to update their experience with periodic spells in a school teaching environment as appropriate;

- Schools chosen for teacher placements must have departments where good practice is the norm and where sufficient support and guidance can be given to trainees. The Executive, in conjunction with the other interested parties, should consider drawing up a list of accredited schools and departments for this purpose and allocating them additional funding.

Probation

3.8 Local authority employers should offer probationers at least a full year of stable employment, involving a strictly limited number of placements, rather than using them for intermittent supply.

Schools should be identified that are able to provide the appropriate support and induction for newly qualified entrants to the profession. Consideration should be given to the idea of designating some schools across the country as "training schools", working in close partnership with TEIs to deliver, on a regional basis, a high-quality and structured introduction to the profession, both during initial training and thereafter. Such an initiative would clearly have resource implications.

Temporary contracts

3.10 The use of temporary contracts for fully qualified teachers should be strictly limited to circumstances where a period of absence is being covered, or where for specific reasons the position being filled is not likely to continue.

Continuing professional development (CPD)

3.15 Courses offered under the heading of CPD should be accredited at national level to ensure their quality and relevance.

Local authorities should review their arrangements for the provision of organised CPD activity in their region to assess its effectiveness.

---

[1] Numbers refer to the relevant paragraphs in the report

The Scottish Executive should establish a national register of approved CPD providers, and review the financing available to schools to support CPD activity.

Every teacher should have an individual CPD plan agreed once a year with his or her immediate manager.

All large primary and secondary schools who have not yet done so should designate a CPD co-ordinator from among the teaching staff to facilitate the management of CPD in the school. For smaller schools, a co-ordinator could be designated for each cluster.

3.16   In view of the importance of CPD, local authorities should, in consultation with the teaching unions, increase the time available for professional development by the equivalent of a further five days a year. This may be undertaken flexibly either outwith the school day or outside the pupil year. This additional commitment should be reflected in the salary structure.

Sabbaticals

3.18   Local authorities should give early and positive consideration to establishing schemes of properly organised sabbaticals, which might be introduced on the basis of a term's break for every ten years spent teaching.

Early retirement and "winding down"

3.25   The pension scheme and schemes for early retirement should be further investigated. The government should also consider a one-off early retirement scheme. Such a scheme could only run successfully if the government is able to provide additional funds, as has been done for other professions in the public sector. Options for "winding down" could, however, make a significant contribution towards improving the provision of supply cover and staff development activity in Scottish schools.

3.26   For the longer term, however, the teaching profession is aware that early retirement costs money, and it may be that the possibility of making larger contributions to the notional pension fund as a means of paying for an entitlement to retirement in advance of the statutory retirement age would find support. Higher contributions are paid by some other public sector employees who retire earlier than teachers. The Committee recommends that this should be discussed with the teachers' unions.

SUPPORT

Senior staff

3.32   All schools of over 500 pupils should have a Senior Administrative Officer reporting to the Headteacher at comparable level to senior teaching staff in the school. In smaller schools, a Senior Administrative Officer should be given responsibility for a cluster of schools.

3.36   As far as the provision of management capacity in general is concerned, the Committee notes that the Scottish Executive is currently consulting on matters relating to school staffing in its review of the Schools (Scotland) Code 1956. In this context, the Committee recommends that the amount of management time available to Headteachers and senior staff should be reviewed.

3.37   The Committee has studied the HMI/Accounts Commission report "Time for Teaching"; endorses its main recommendations; and would wish to see all those involved give immediate attention to how best to put them into practice.

Clerical staff

3.38   There should always be at least one member of staff in each school able to deal with routine emergencies and contact parents during the pupil day.

Social inclusion

3.40   The Committee considers it important that where increased demands arise from the social inclusion policy, these should be adequately resourced.   This may have implications for staffing levels in schools. The Committee recommends that where the tasks involved do not require teachers' expertise and are more appropriate to other professionals, such as social and health workers and therapists, such professionals should be made available.   Teachers will play their part, but it is not reasonable to add to the burdens of that profession by imposing tasks for which others are better fitted. It should also be underlined that parents, too, have an important part to play in supporting the work of the school.   The removal of any doubt about the government's understanding of the implications of these matters would do much to reassure the teaching profession.

3.41   Effective action to tackle the problem of pupil indiscipline is essential not only to reduce the stress on teachers, but also in the interests of the majority of pupils for whom behaviour is not a problem.   Teachers, parents, local authorities and the Executive all have a role to play; and the Committee recommends that the Executive carry out an appraisal of its policies in this regard, particularly the resources allocated to them.

Information technology

3.42   Every school or cluster of schools should have ready access to fully-trained personnel with the appropriate technical expertise and knowledge of the application of technology in the educational context.

Supply cover

3.43   The Scottish Executive and local authorities should review the way that supply cover is provided and managed across Scotland, and consider how it might be improved, for example by the constitution of standing teams of permanent peripatetic teachers.

Classroom assistants

3.45   The number of trained classroom assistants in the primary sector be increased substantially beyond the current target, with the objective that there should be at least one classroom assistant for every three primary classes in Scotland.   In the secondary sector a similar cadre of trained para-professionals should be provided, particularly in S1 and S2 and in appropriate subject areas, to help with the preparation of materials and any other tasks which will enable teachers to concentrate on their teaching duties.

Section 4: Career structure

4.10   The Committee recommends moving to a four-band structure as soon as practicable. This should have the following elements:

- a main grade for classroom teachers, to incorporate all existing unpromoted teachers and Senior Teachers. In general, existing Assistant Principal Teachers would fall into this grade: but in some cases, where their posts carry significant management responsibilities, they might be assimilated into the middle management grade. Within the main grade, there should be significantly improved prospects for reward for teachers without the need to move into a management post.

- a middle management grade. The Committee recognises the key role played by Principal Teachers and recommends that the grade should continue. This grade would encompass all existing Principal Teachers and probably a limited number of Assistant Principal Teachers. This grade would be mainly responsible for subject and guidance leadership within the secondary sector, as at present: but it should also be possible for Principal Teacher posts to be deployed more flexibly, and for Principal Teacher posts to be deployed in the primary sector, as one way of addressing the need for more management capacity. These choices should be made at local level, in the light of local needs.

- a single senior management grade, to be called Depute Headteacher, encompassing existing Assistant Headteachers and Depute Headteachers. The creation of a single grade would reflect the essentially collegiate nature of the job of a senior management team.

- a Headteacher grade. The Committee considers that the job of Headteacher, with the significant representational and leadership functions and accountability it carries in all sizes of school, should be considered as a separate band within the profession.

4.12-13 In order to recognise and reward excellence in the classroom and encourage continuing professional development within the teaching profession, the Committee also recommends that the Scottish Executive, together with the GTC and TEIs and consulting local authority employers and the teaching unions, should develop by the end of this year a national programme and standards for Chartered Teacher status to be implemented by 1 April 2002. This programme should be open to all experienced classroom teachers. The Committee expects Chartered Teacher status to be within the reach of a significant majority of teachers; and anticipates that they would be motivated to achieve it. It would constitute a personal achievement, rather than a post. The programme would require completion of a challenging and structured programme of relevant and accredited CPD, over a period of four years, aimed at improving teaching and other professional skills. Progress towards, and achievement of, Chartered Teacher status would be rewarded with additional salary points. Once acquired, teachers would keep the status and the associated salary points if they transferred to another school. Acquisition of Chartered Teacher status would not involve taking on any additional management responsibility beyond that of a maingrade teacher.

4.14-15 Furthermore, the Committee recommends the introduction, on the same timescale, of a more demanding programme for Advanced Chartered Teacher status for which all Chartered Teachers would be able to apply. It would involve a programme of CPD focusing on development of classroom practice through research and advanced learning, in conjunction with the TEIs. Achievement of Advanced Chartered Teacher status would be subject to external assessment of classroom expertise. As for the Chartered Teacher, progress towards, and achievement of, Advanced Chartered Teacher status would attract additional salary; Advanced Chartered Teachers could earn as much as or more than Principal Teachers. Although ACT status is intended to be an end in itself for the dedicated and experienced teacher who wishes to develop his or her career in the classroom, Advanced Chartered Teachers would be expected to make a wide contribution towards the development of teaching and learning in their own schools and beyond, with particular emphasis on training and mentoring of junior colleagues.

Section 5: Pay

(Our recommendations should be uprated to reflect the outcome of the current negotiation in the SJNC on a cost-of-living increase to apply from 1 April 2000)

5.31   The starting salary for all graduate entrants should be increased to £17,000.

Probationer teachers should receive an increase of £500 after their first year's service, and a further £1,500 on completion of the probationary period, so that the starting salary for a fully qualified main grade teacher is £19,000.

The scale for main grade teachers should proceed in five equal steps to a new increased maximum of £26,000 for a fully experienced teacher.

Beyond that maximum, teachers embarking on the programme to acquire Chartered Teacher status described in the preceding section of this report should proceed by further annual increments of £750, (subject to satisfactory progress through the programme) to a salary for a certified Chartered Teacher of £29,000.

Teachers wishing to proceed to Advanced Chartered Teacher status should receive further annual increments of £1,250 over the course of their four-year programme to a maximum for a certified Advanced Chartered Teacher of £34,000.

Principal Teachers should be paid on a short, three-point range going from £30,000 to £35,000, with placement to depend on school roll.

The new Depute Headteacher grade should be paid on a four-point range from £30,000 to £44,000, depending on school roll. In view of the collegiate nature of work in the senior management team within a school, Depute Headteachers within the same school should all receive the same salary.

Headteachers should be paid on a nine-point range going from £36,000 to £61,500, depending on school roll.

5.37   Headteachers should have the flexibility to award additional payments of up to £1,000 on a time-limited basis to Principal or maingrade teachers in recognition of such additional tasks. The budgetary arrangements for schools should be made more flexible to allow Headteachers the discretion to do so. Any additional payments should not, however, be consolidated and should not normally exceed two years in duration.

5.38   In schools too small to justify a permanent Depute, the Headteacher should also have the flexibility to make an additional payment to another member of staff for deputising in his or her absence, without prejudice to the existing arrangements for "acting-up" during more prolonged absences.

5.39   Similarly, Head Teachers should have the discretion to make modest additional payments to maingrade teachers for activities going above and beyond their normal responsibilities.

5.40   More generally, within the context of arrangements for devolved school management it should be possible for Headteachers, in co-operation with the local authority, to vary the management structure and deployment of posts within a school in the light of changing circumstances. The Committee recommends that the Scottish Executive and local authorities examine current practice with a view to facilitating such flexibility.

Section 6: Conditions of service

6.6   In future core issues such as pay, main duties, overall working time, sickness and maternity leave, and discipline should continue to be determined nationally. However, it is for consideration whether other conditions of service should be agreed at national or local level. The Committee notes that Task Group 4 of the Millennium Review proposed an extension of the scope for local negotiation; and recommends that such flexibility should apply in any future framework.

Teachers' duties

6.12   The duties of all teachers should include: teaching assigned classes, together with the associated preparation and correction; developing the school curriculum; assessing, recording and reporting on the work of pupils; preparing pupils for examinations, and sharing responsibility for administering them; offering advice and guidance to pupils; promoting and safeguarding the health, welfare and safety of pupils; working in partnership with parents and other professional colleagues; undertaking appropriate continuing professional development in order to maintain and improve   skills and competences; participating with colleagues in planning, raising attainment, school self-improvement, and individual review; and contributing, together with colleagues, towards the good order and wider life of the school.

6.13   Teachers who are promoted to Principal Teacher and above should in addition have explicit responsibility for the leadership, good management and strategic direction of their department, faculty or for the school (depending on their level); curriculum development and quality assurance; the development of school policy for the behaviour management of pupils; the management and guidance of junior professional colleagues, in particular those still on probation; the review and appraisal of colleagues' performance; the provision of advice to junior colleagues, as appropriate, on their career development and CPD needs; and, as appropriate, links with the wider community.

6.14   Responsibilities must, however, be balanced by rights. The Committee considers that all teachers should have the right to expect an enabling framework of resources, organisation, time management, strategic planning, consultation, personnel and professional support, high quality CPD and support from parents to assist them in carrying out their responsibilities.

6.15   The Committee recommends that broad descriptions along these lines should replace the existing detailed provisions of the national scheme; and that any more detailed job descriptions should be decided at local level on the basis of specific needs relating to individual posts.

Workload and working time

6.18   The Scottish Executive, when considering any new initiative of whatever kind, should ensure that the profession is properly consulted on its design; and should evaluate its likely impact on workload. Where this evaluation reveals that a significant increase is likely, the Executive should consider the allocation of additional resources to implement the initiative, or should defer its introduction. Once initiatives have been introduced, their implementation should be kept under regular review so that unintended consequences in terms of workload can be addressed. Moreover, there should be a mechanism within the Executive for co-ordinating the various activities which will impact on schools, with a view to ensuring coherence, consistency and the greatest possible degree of streamlining.

6.19   The Executive should commission an independent "bureaucracy audit", to be carried out by independent consultants, to look at:

- the amount, form and frequency of information required from schools by the Scottish Executive Education Department, Her Majesty's Inspectorate and local authorities;

- the benefit it generates for pupils, parents and policy-makers;

- and to make recommendations on the design of processes with a view to reducing the burden on teachers arising from information demands.

Working hours

6.28-31   35 hours should continue to be the basis for the contractual week. Within the 35-hour contract week, 30 hours would be allocated to "core" activities comprising class contact and preparation and correction. The balance, five hours, should be available for the range of other collective activities contributing to the wider life of the school, to be decided by the staff in each school on a collegiate basis, led by the Headteacher as overall manager and the person ultimately accountable for the activities of the school. The use of this collective time should in principle be decided annually. It might be necessary to deploy it flexibly over the course of the school year, for example to deal with peaks of activity at assessment time or at the start of the session. Equally, in some cases it might not be necessary to use the equivalent of the whole 5 hours. The key point is that collegiate activities should be planned, agreed, deployed and used collectively for the benefit of the whole school.

6.36   There should be 30 hours for core activities in primary schools, the same as for secondaries; and maximum class contact time should also be the same. We recognise that this will take some time to achieve, and that it may require some additional teachers in the primary sector. In this context, we would also see advantage in providing a greater number of specialist staff to the primary schools, perhaps on a cluster basis, in recognition of the breadth of the curriculum that now has to be covered; and we recommend that this option be examined urgently.

The working year

6.40   A further five days or their equivalent be allocated to continuing professional development. This time should be made available flexibly either from the time beyond the pupil year or from time beyond the 35 hour week.

Class sizes

6.43-44 We do not propose any changes to the existing maximum class sizes as part of our report. We do, however, recognise the sensitivity of the issue; and recommend that the Scottish Executive commission independent research into the relationship between class sizes and individual educational attainment.

Absence cover

6.45   The existing national agreement has in many cases been overtaken, and should be deleted.

Transfer of temporary teachers to the permanent staff

6.46   The Committee is concerned about the widespread use of temporary contracts: but has reservations about the effectiveness of the current provision of the scheme of conditions of service as this issue. It therefore recommends that the provision be deleted in any new national scheme of conditions of service: but also[2] that use of temporary contracts should be limited to the strict minimum.

Section 7: Ensuring quality

7.7   The Scottish Executive, in close co-operation with the local authorities and consulting the teaching unions, should take immediate steps to introduce universal review procedures in line with best practice identified across Scotland.

7.11   The Committee strongly urges the Executive to press ahead, in close co-operation with other interested parties, with the definition of national standards for capability and the issuance of guidance on their use.

7.15   The Committee urges the relevant parties to agree on a new framework for disciplinary procedures as quickly as possible.

Section 8: Future negotiating mechanism

8.18   Teachers' pay should be determined by collective bargaining, in the form of a national bargaining committee. This committee should generally work on an annual cycle, but with the discretion to negotiate two- or three-year settlements should it so choose.

There should, however, be flexibility for local negotiation between individual authorities and local unions, on the whole range of issues identified in the report of Task Group 4 of the Millennium Review, subject to notifying the national bargaining committee for approval on core issues.

The bargaining committee should be composed of representatives of the local authority employers; of the teaching unions, including the Headteachers' associations not currently represented in the SJNC; and of the Scottish Executive, as full participants in the negotiation;

Agreements reached in this body need not be enacted in statute.   Employment law should provide sufficient safeguards against abuse.

In addition to the bargaining committee, the Minister for Children and Education should establish a small independent body which should carry out a three-yearly review of salaries, whose reports and recommendations should be delivered to all parties in the bargaining committee and made public.   This review should compare the evolution of teachers' salaries against a range of comparator occupations over the preceding period, and should incorporate a pay levels check against a range of other occupations, based on a job evaluation exercise; it should also examine developments in relation to the supply of teachers.   The body should have discretion to look at how conditions of service are operating, and whether adjustments are required; and should be able to submit reports and detailed recommendations to the bargaining committee for consideration.

---

[2]   See paragraph 3.10

Terms of reference

The Committee is requested to inquire widely into:

(a) how teachers' pay, promotion structures and conditions of service should be changed in order to ensure a committed, professional and flexible teaching force which will secure high and improving standards of school education for all children in Scotland into the new Millennium; and

(b) the future arrangements for determining teachers' pay and conditions in Scotland following the removal of the statutory basis of the Scottish Joint Negotiating Committee (School Education) now proposed by the Scottish Executive;

and to make recommendations.

In framing its recommendations, the Committee:

(a) must have regard to public expenditure issues including affordability and the implications of the Government's inflation target for the general level of public sector pay settlements; and

(b) should take into account the following principles:

- teachers' pay should be at a level to recruit, retain and motivate high quality teaching staff;

- there should be a clear and demonstrable link between additional pay for teachers and revised conditions and working practices, which meet the need for modernisation and higher standards;

- there should be opportunities for career advancement for teachers, especially teachers of acknowledged excellence, who wish to continue to deploy their skills in the classroom;

- the structure of pay and conditions of service should be designed to promote and reward effectiveness in both teaching and school management; and

- management structures in schools should be sufficiently flexible to meet changing needs and challenges while ensuring effective delivery of the daily responsibilities of each school.

In conducting its inquiry, the Committee may wish to commission research and invite evidence from teachers and teachers' representatives, local authorities, the Scottish Executive, parents' representatives, further and higher education, industry, commerce and other parties interested in school education. It should also seek to draw on examples of best practice from elsewhere in the public and private sectors and overseas.

The Committee's recommendations:

(a) may cover any or all of the issues set out in the SJNC management side's offer to the teachers' side dated 20 August 1999; but

(b) Should not address the question of any pay increase for 1999 which will remain a matter for the management and staff sides of the SJNC (SE).

The Committee

Professor Gavin McCrone CB - Visiting Professor, Edinburgh University Management School since 1994. Deputy Chairman of the Lothian University Hospitals Trust, and a member of the Parliamentary Boundary Commission for Scotland.

Mr Alan Campbell - Chief Executive, Aberdeenshire Council since 1995.

Mr Campbell Christie CBE - (Former General Secretary of the Scottish Trade Union Congress); Member of the EU Economic and Social Committee; Board Member of Forth Valley Acute Hospital Trust, Scottish Enterprise, British Waterways and Falkirk Football and Athletic Club; Chairman, Lothian Trade Union and Community Resource Centre.

Professor Bob Elliott - Professor of Economics, University of Aberdeen since 1990.

Mr David Hutchison - Civil Engineer and Director of Cadogan Consultants (consulting engineers, Glasgow). President of the Scottish School Boards Association since 1995. One of the Secretary of State's nominees on the General Teaching Council for Scotland.

Ms Patricia McCall - Headteacher, Campie Primary School, Musselburgh since 1993.

Mr Norrie McLeod - General Manager (Personnel), Standard Life Assurance Company since 1991.

Mrs Anne Mulgrew - Headteacher, St Andrew's High School, East Kilbride since 1986.

Secretary: Alisdair McIntosh

Designed and produced by Tactica Solutions B13173 5/00